POWER STEERING 2

By M. J. SCOTT
USA

Copyright 2016 M. J. Scott

Published by Daniel Wetta Publishing

Other Titles by M. J. Scott:
Power Steering
Journey into Fulfillment
Time On the Turn

For more information about the author and her books, please visit author website at www.danielwetta.com/author-m-j-scott/

Cover design: Daniel Wetta

Deep in the Forest of Thought

Imagine...Rhythms...Life

Dedication

To the readers of Power Steering 2, for their time in giving the intuitive an opportunity to be its own adventure. To everyone who uses his or her personal gifts with deep sensitivity to others. Thank you for joining on this highway of wonder.

Table of Contents

Chapter 1: Power Train

IT'S YOUR WORLD

When world news tonight reaches the eyes and ears of the electronic waves, how do we relate?

There's another "It's Your World" spinning when you open the circuits of meeting like-hearts-and-minds, giving them a sharing space. It may be in the phone call of voice-closeness that unites lives in an instant of understanding.

"It's Your World" - how broad its spinning shape is up to you. Allow glimmers of light to shine in the friendships of bonding and caring. Your space and time are an open world's door. Allowing this door to open wide or a bit ajar is always your choice, but a door is two-way. Don't forget to allow families and friends to come through the doors and windows of your life. Sharing a morsel of enrichment or laughter through the air waves transmits moments of healthy joy.

Today, a big bowl of Cheerios was waiting on the kitchen counter of a family who brought a visual delight.

"Cheerio!" Today is special, whatever your profession. Allow cheer to brighten your world. It will be brighter because you are aware.

In my day today, like-minds will meet, and then after the electronic door provides exit, I'll transform learning into doing. Opportunities are always in the seeking or in the incubating thought. Seize them for the Creative Channel.

Joining this merry-go-round of our world in slow motion, we share a space to just live and breathe in God's Great Goodness. It's Your World; it's Our World; it's God's World of spinning happiness.

Wow! A showering of blessings with just a little burst of energy from spigot to raindrops of springtime.

"Hello!"

THE VULNERABLE US, OR OUR BACK BONE

Power Steering releases the emergency brakes of vulnerability. This allows a surprisingly voluntary sharing of life, relating writer and reader to a Higher Power for guidance.

A gentle opening of emotions permits everyone to fathom the kinship of life that exists. Thoughts released into the ethers of life form clouds of greatness that have never been explored.

The mind is powerful, and it must be exercised as with weights in fitness centers. Oh, you think this writer is being daring, and why not? Living is a daring opportunity in the potential of everyone. There's no time for depression and drugs to submerge creativity like a nuclear submarine.

Go ahead: Let the power of the moment in silence awaken you. Be prepared for the flow of thought and motion to become new friends. Well, for goodness' sake, that's quite a task, you think. But guess what? Your emergency brakes aren't needed, unless you are parked on a hill of fear.

Enough said, perhaps, but what fun to be the signer of a new physical and mental constitution! Even Mr. Jefferson in his Monticello study might smile, and also General Lee in his photograph so proudly taken from a painting in history that is all mine.

The light of magic could be sitting right on your dresser stand, and you never before let it shine. So turn on your personal ignition for Power Steering to be your guest.

THE INTUITIVE CALL

Fascination enriches our lines of thought in simple letters of call. Yet it may be recall that is also potent. Responding to both may be powered by an invisible urge to reach satisfaction.

What is satisfaction? Is it that link between the now and the ever-elusive solution to life?

The intuitive reveals that mysterious presence of purpose and goal of each day, not those in the far off calendar pages.

Our pathway may be filled with stumbling of footsteps or the stumbling and fumbling for the essence of truth.

Essence of life is a fragrance in the awesome beauty of springtime that emerges in the oozing sap of trees. We breathe youth and start on ageless searches of discovery.

Suddenly, the wordless feelings that can't be measured become the pinnacle: the indescribable beckoning of the intuitive to share the gift of life for others to find. It is a discovery in time spinning subtly away, but it can be caught and released from its captor's net.

The intuitive call can bring time to slow motion and release the fulfillment of relaxation that enables body, mind and spirit to be united.

Skip with the youthfulness of springtime, laugh with the joy of life, and find the revelation of seasons to be your own enormous blessing. The tools of living are your personal bequeath inside God's special delivery package of rebirth. The intuitive call is personal, individual, and a treasure in discovery!

THE ELUSIVE LOVE

A word sown into the fiber of birth, but left to be discovered.

Positions of life change with the experiences we encounter, from warm arms of parents to reassurances and compliments when we learn to talk and walk.

Then, as cycles of growth bring changes, the word "love" seems to melt like butter on the stove. There's no one telling you that the word will heal wounds or that it also can burn. Burn units in hospitals graft skin to repair scars, but only time crossing calendars can heal the inner wounds of love lost.

Elusive love can't be placed in a treasure box from the dust of recall. It is a joy-filled love that can't be ribbon tied, but it can radiate inner yearnings that begin to build an individual definition of what this beautiful word means to you. Love can be that silent veil that lies below the surface for others to feel and recognize as their own mystery.

Love is a mysterious thread holding life in gentle sanity.

It plants itself in sparkling eyes, crinkly smiles and the indefinable wonder of living.

The keys to ignite this strongest element in the stream of life are in the hands of a guardian angel who taps our shoulder. We heave a sigh and say, "At last!"

Artisans of all times strive to express or show this elusive creation. Sensitivity to the real enabled through the Power Steering of God's mighty plan. The strength and power of elusive love can lift our human condition to a higher form of life. The keys are within every heart for each person to find. Books are written, plays are acted, and music is sung to express this majesty of God's great grace.

"PEACE!"

HIDDEN LOVE

Every child of God populating our world has a fundamental need. While exploring life, at some point each discovers that the deepest need is to be loved.

Observing all shades of eyes in the people we meet, we see that hidden within their sparkling or clouded expressions lies mystery. In an instant of perception, we find the hidden dimensions of the other person in a new level of realization.

But often we don't give another thought, as the hurrying feet carry these earthly pedestrians on their ways. To stop and think of our planet of humanity opens a wealth of enchantment because we see submerged behind the expressions of our earthly angels their hidden gifts of love.

Often love is not taught in the home. Perhaps there are those who never thought that this neglected element would be innately received in just a hug, a picking-up, or a caring for basic needs. Love needs to be shared verbally to give children confidence to pass through the growth cycle of adolescence. The recognition of love has immense power!

The demonstration of this powerhouse comes when our teenagers find this big hurdle of adolescence to face. We push the kids into the rash of activities of sports, music, study and other things that exhaust their energies. They have no model of introspection. They feel bewildered or angry, and they hide their need for love.

Justifying over-activities to carry them through those precarious years - Can they learn the benefits of controlling desires so that they might hold on and reach maturity safely? Stirred-up hormonal emotions stoke uncontrollable fires that reach passionate heights. Will they understand their inner demands and confusing passions with no guidance about how to use restraint?

Let's teach the youth to know that their soul mate is the ultimate partner. The trial-and-error search brings the great determiner of fate. Dare we be so bold as to say that true love awaits in the wings for everyone?

"Happy Birthday to everyone!"

Feel deep joy unleased.

PERSONALLY YOURS

What is the personal "you" like? Are you the sum of feelings based on your own sense of purpose, or are you described by how you have given totally to others? What time is your own and only for you? Does numbness depart and feeling return? Is it your life, or are others in charge? Questions flow, and in the slow seeking of answers and acknowledgements, the personal "you" begins to appear.

Have you been drained of energy with no time to recharge? Stop! This is burying yourself. You are missing awareness that could come suddenly. It is unable to be exposed, because the movement of time has corroded the chain of events necessary for its release.

"Mirror, mirror on the wall," is you! Have you rediscovered your dynamic personality that was locked away with what seemed a lost key? Well, pick up the key, turn on the engine and get rolling!

Your very own God-given gifts are ready to be exercised and shared for a waiting world. The role you serve will make a difference! Your personality is unique, you are unique, and the uniqueness of every soul must be discovered!

YOU ARE ALWAYS FUN!

What is fun in the experience of others? It may have a dictionary definition, but that can't possibly explain the elation of driving your first car. Was it a convertible with the wind in your face and freedom of the open road? Glance at the speedometer and hit the accelerator for a ride in the country. Now that's one exciting, action-filled bit of fun!

Fun can be the chatter of friends sharing stories. Fun can be feeling serendipity wrapped up in a sunbeam. Taking off the wrist watch and letting time melt into the veins of human encounter. Some try to sell fun, but it's truly a self-discovered dimension of living.

It is frightening to watch a "60 Minutes" documentary and find that the heroin pill or syringe has become prevalent in the search for fun within the culture of town and country. "You are always fun" brings a big responsibility to just be yourself with all the authentic little bits of life that you share with others. The genuineness of being you. And if humor runs through your engine, then let it roll on. Life is too short to skip the humaneness of living and extending love. There's a connection when heaven and earth meet in an instant, and it brings the peace of being. It doesn't take entertainment. It just can be sitting on a fencepost and laughing at the October jack-o-lantern.

Written in the shadow of a rain-stained window, but fun has also felt like the candle burning brightly at the junction of mind and heart. Power Steering allows for a glorious fun-filled day.

WONDER

Reaching for a pad of paper, I salvage a thought nearly lost in the search.

Why are fascinations so far away in the call of the mountains of indigenous people? Is it the cry of the land once hidden or deserted and having moved beyond? Could it be the refugees struggling through the winter winds that have carried their yearnings here? Questions without answers.

Measurements of love!

Blessings of hot chocolate and soothing face on the pillow of night: these have collided with pen, hope and love!

Thank you, Lord, for your grace to breathe, to feel and appreciate life as it continues to unwind in great surges of wonder.

The clock keeps climbing past seconds into minutes, and I sense destiny in its proclamation. How far will power steering take each of us?

Blessings of creation to be recognized!

URGINGS

Perhaps you have no interest at all, except we all have urgings to proceed. Whatever this urge may be, I can only guess that yours is private! So are mine, except when the nighttime sleep ceases and the rush to write becomes the strongest.

Urgings are the inner-most thoughts radiating outward to a needy world hungry for encouragement. So Power Steering once again becomes the little wizard of urging to be recognized.

The wonder races ahead of the individual and wants an explanation to be ready. Are you ready? Does it say, "Go back to school and open the books of unfinished degrees? Or, walk right up to an electronic door and pass through into a new profession? That's the wonderful part of freedom of choice. You see, urgings are the little stimulators for deeper contemplation. Challenges lie just beyond forethought. They are negotiated with reason, time and determination.

Let the creative urgings rise to the heights. Revisit intentions for a particular goal. Being driven by this dynamic urging, you will make the world a better and stronger place because you are present and ready, now!

MINDSWEPT

Daring to enter this page of sweeping dreams may leave us all with another dimension of awareness.

Triggers of thought even more powerful than a gun. The gun closes out a scenario if the trigger is ignited, but the mind sweeping thoughts can live forever.

Try a beautiful bottle of artisan water purchased from a book store that cradles thoughts. The hibiscus of hot-pink splendor attracts the eye with more than the wet quenching of a drink. It lures dreams into faraway places on a search for the tropical paradise or utopia. Mind-swept thoughts could bring dreams into action.

Slip into a photograph or painting and join for an instant what that creative artist might have been thinking. Then, "Wow!" You could miniaturize the idea to fit a memory cell, and then move on to explore another mind adventure.

On and on...Stroking a little or large statue, you feel the coolness of the marble. The longer it remains in the embrace of your hand, the warmer it becomes. In that mind-swept moment you may have felt the touch and chisel of Michelangelo.

Now arrives the awareness of the relaxing moments when "mind-swept" has cleared the tension from your own breathing self.

The joy of finding a new level of thinking just below the surface.

Thank you for joining this author into the mind-swept adventure that requires no passport. Perhaps your adventure makes you serious to fly on for real.

For a moment, it seemed to have stopped the clock. Your mental adventure became a time saver, mind saver, and life preserver!

"Thank you, Lord!"

DROWNING

Efforts to not drown in the schedules of daily life seem to be forgotten. So let's try putting on a life preserver and omitting some of the nonessentials on the "to do" list for today.

We always see troubling scenes of drowning on the beaches, because the reckless ones haven't paid attention to their inner warnings. They dare the waves of strong tides and think, "I'll take the next big one!" But the reverse is true!

The strong storms rip through lives in the weather patterns of great surprise. The heights of these waves create crisis. Hope might drown, but it can build again.

Cancelling an appointment on the day before its schedule may create an inconvenience, but it may become a blessing in disguise. The depletion of energies is a malady of our 24/7 culture that pressures us to move ahead. Let's just slow this momentum a wee bit and think about what makes us relaxed and happy. Think of others in your life who are blessed by your being with them now. Whatever the circumstances, try treating life as your gift to self and others. Yes, I know that we are often nagged by the old feeling of being "selfish", but that burdens the yoke of the creative heart. A temperate climate is not just the weather outside; it may be also the inner weather tempered for the soul to live to its fullest potential.

I just evaluated a wonderful photography course in a seated room, and now I will take moments set aside to go roaming outside for the perfect three-dimensional shot. Photo shoots provide glorious moments when the focus is only on the subject and self has been forgotten. Well, except for pushing down the shutter button.

Swimming in your unique creative expression is the life preserver making it possible to bubble to the heights. Enjoy!

POWER STEERING - ON REGULAR BREW

Life keeps spilling over in blessings as the back-up camera revealed today. It showed clearly a lady backing up in a big SUV. We had the good fortune of an unwanted meeting being averted!

Previous to that, I had a great conversation with a young cashier: "You are always on duty!" "Oh yes, I work full-time and go to school full-time." "What are you studying? "I don't know what major I will declare yet, but I'm terribly good in math." "Terrific! And in management too! I'll check on you again!" I looked at the product coupon he handed me for a future shopping trip: "Pledge!" The name was perfect for ending our conversation.

Another favorite, eggs and toast, placed next on the noontime list. My favorite nook on the edge of town and country was selected with comfort. A sweet young teen escorted by her trainer arrived to take my order. She returned with the plate oven-hot, a perfect biscuit, and scrambled eggs with cheese. She asked, "Is everything alright?" "Oh my, yes, and is this your first day?" She nodded, and I graced her with 4.0 and A+. "You are great!" Mattie was her name.

On our stroll through life, we are meant to encourage the younger generation and introduce ourselves to them.

Reaching for a condiment jelly to make the biscuit like a breakfast dessert, I chose the apple butter by Smuckers. First and foremost! It blended into a happy memory of having gone to college with one of the heirs. Life is rich in such bountiful hometown recalls.

A little prologue can tell you that our "Mattie" will be one of our budding nurses who loves helping people. This is an assurance that our world is in God's hands with His angels helping people. Thank you, Power Steering, for my new friend!

This has been food for mind and soul today. Try this menu of delight! I hate to leave this environment. Then, calling a "Hello" to another waitress by name, I was greeted by her return with five maple syrup containers. The little thing of recognizing her made her tray lighter. It's the little things that lighten a life.

Now it's time to move along.

HEART OF TIME

Within the pulse-beat of time, unmeasured by human eye, there is an all-knowing within that comes from Higher Power.

We needn't worry about this within our human breast, as Higher Power holds the length of destiny. To wonder is good, as the awareness brings focus to our purpose. Then we rise above the everyday-calendar page to the satisfaction of striving for the best.

Our focus reflects in the eyes of each beholder and their clear and penetrating interest. We are aware of our special guides for the day. We find ourselves opening doors for strangers and rediscovering familiar faces from the past. Each encounter is delightful and immeasurable in depth. There's a touch to remind us of right place and time towards destiny.

The impulse to judge will not appear on our calendar. Instead, the unexpected again thrives and stirs our hearts.

"Thank you, Lord, for showing me to preserve breath and heart in order to receive energy to experience these precious moments with others."

GEARING UP FOR ADVENTURE

This spell-binding reference can lead to a real mental gymnastics spin!

Will we be deep sea diving and following coordinates to pin-point ancient ship wrecks? Or is the image one of planning a safari to some exotic jungle? It's all in the mind sweeping away barriers to the mysterious and undiscovered parts of our inner desires. No writer or teacher can show us the pathway. We must open the door to a new surrounding or to opportunities that may reveal to us fantastic new horizons.

The greatest adventure may be the pounding of your heart for a soul mate, the very one that God purposed for your destiny. It's all so unexplained in the where, who, when and how; dependent, also, upon your willingness to travel into awareness of your inner wholeness. The soulmate love is the deepest kind of love. It roots infinitely deeper than the physical attraction. There is inner, spiritual yearning that has spewed from the crest of the Divine. To encounter this is the beginning of a capital adventure. Are you game for knowing at first sight this is possible? Your own adventure begins with climbing into the spacecraft of Love.

Still spinning?

IT'S A WOW!

When time and space meet on the edge of dawn, it's a "Wow" moment! Grasping this creative light is to receive a gift that spirit prepares for the unsuspecting.

The energy that embraces the newness of day is powerful and opens the feelings discovered within of inner delight.

All who ask to receive these creative moments find the next steps to the acts of faith, hope and love. These miracles abound, and they surround our lives if we allow them to imprint our streams of consciousness.

This mystical "Wow!" becomes an audible expression of awareness. Conscious thoughts can be swept away without a brush stroke, replaced by intentions revealed and recorded by pen or keystroke for the sight of author and reader. The elusive breath of peace calms the restless soul, and from that blessed state flows an abundance of peaceful expression.

Each day is a page turning to a point of no return. The day must be given a space to recognize the importance of greeting and hugging and being thankful for each experience. Have you met the "Wow!" in your daily walk? Maybe it is in listening to a dove coo: a bird's song that holds a charm of meaning. It makes you stop somewhere in your tracks just to embrace a new feeling!

There's power in the moment, so allow its presence to ring a new bell of courage to speak, act and give. Remnants not of cloth, but of a stream of happiness that swells and moves: Another gift of discovery!

Are we able to absorb it all without a shout of "Wow," expressing emotion for this creative stroke of wonder, delight and praise? (Perhaps today all I will do is type these flowing thoughts before washing the grime from my car and then easing down the highway. Away!)

Heart almost stopping...

"Thank you, Lord!".

DENIAL

Little miniscule thoughts that want to drift to the heights....

The moment released, and they almost disappeared without allowing their purpose to be expressed. They could have been denied.

Perhaps, when the weaving of words is denied, it's like sticking a little hidden treasure into a closet already filled with like bounties.

Oh my, closets of unworn clothes and unexpressed thoughts are left to hang side by side and crushed by another hanger placed on the rail!

Altar of moments so precious.

CONFIDENCE

This is a powerful word in the living of everyday, and it can be recognized in the pattern of behaviors.

Confidence is like a nutritional performance of everything that speaks your name. It's the way you hold your shoulders, head and smile, for starters. Skip the frowns! Those cause wrinkles too soon. Confidence can also lie in the signature of writing for those who read the handwriting signs.

Do you wonder why people buy certain cars by name or design? This is another attribute of confidence shown. The style of clothing, be it casual or a touch of the formal resort, is always an expression of you. Sometimes it comes from the subconscious self, speaking out silently, but, for others, it's just the way you are. Okay, it's the way we are!

A beautiful example of these colorful little thoughts is the lady entering the walkway to the post office. She was wearing a crown of white hair (a la natural), trim slacks and a white sweater bearing a flourish of the American flag. She smiled at my car. It seemed to meet her approval. That felt nice. She chatted with a gentleman in line and radiated that glorious smile. Suddenly, I couldn't help but say to her, "You have the most beautiful smile." She responded, to my surprise, with a returning compliment.

Upon her leaving the desk, I gave her my author business card as a thanks for just "being." She was delighted, and it seemed to me that the contagion of enthusiasm was a measure of growing confidence for each of us.

Yes, confidence is a measure of our feeling of self-worth, and we all need to manage it in its stages of growing. Sometimes it is reflected in our choice not to do something. For example, a moment ago the doorbell rang with a strong shrill sound. The unexpected sound and the car in the driveway just weren't my signal to answer the door. Appointments are for preparedness, and the first morning coffee hadn't quite hit the pipeline.

Enjoying your chosen purpose in the adventure of work and play is a gift of confidence. Its success is marked with a smile.

Confidence is daring to be vulnerable and open to this world called life. However, this disclaimer is important: Watch out for the people who run red lights, forget the pedestrian crossings, and don't respect the white tipped canes. Confidence embraces acting responsibly, not recklessly. So take heed of the service dogs who walk with confidence, guiding their masters.

We are all fortunate, really. Thank you for sharing these written moments with me.

Chapter 2: The Power of Emotions

IN TOUCH WITH SELF

The title may seem so selfish at first glance, but, in a second thought, do we ever give this an open door to explore?

What does the intuitive say to this self within the boundaries of height, weight and address? Simple, silly little nothings get ignored, because self runs a race everyday with the should-have-done or the should-do lists.

When the kitty comes to say goodnight, he receives a happy toenail scratch and then gets a tempting seafood-medley treat. It's the listening to the little crunch and soft whiskers tickling the hand that makes keeping in touch special. Each of us is special and unique on our spinning planet. The Creator of All has given each of us tools of sensitivity to discover the little things that lead to blessings by the big things.

Perhaps this would have never been written if my link to the outside world hadn't stopped this afternoon. I write first by hand. There was no computer to distract me. Tonight, the computer is still able to light up and receive incoming emails, but the sending out is on the refusal mode. Tomorrow may bring answers, but tonight only the green package of kitty treats is my reminder that it's never too late to discover self. You'll find it a glorious treat to meet yourself. How about that for a little goodnight wish?

All systems are on off, and eyelids too are waiting for a closing down.

P.S. The computer remedy was a new battery required in the wireless keyboard. We, too, need to battery-up for energizing!

IF

If there's a song in your heart, sing it! If there's a tear on your cheek, brush it free. If you feel lost, then find a friend for comfort. The world is filled with "ifs," and it's hard to distinguish the honest and the counterfeit. We'll build a house if we have the blue-prints. The blue prints were already hidden from view and only came into view when these were given away. Perhaps the intention to impress with the plan is more important than the carrying to fruition.

The wild world of "ifs" can be a burden or a blessing. I wonder where you have found these two little letters that carry promise? Why even mention this small word? Well, it can carry you to the heights of joy, or it just might become a cliff-hanger. I've been to the top of the mountain to find the beautiful view. But be careful of the valley after the descent. Look always for the positive side of thought, and reach for the hand of the Great Comforter. *If* you get caught in the rubble of negativism, just start a new climb up the other side of the mountain.

Sunrise and sunsets are glorious...if you believe.

CPR

If happiness has taken a holiday and suddenly returns as if from a space-walk, you may need CPR. The experience can be like a brain-freeze resulting from swiftly consuming an icy "Big Gulp" of a 7-11 drink. Swallowing is in question. Suddenly you are breathing in gasps and gulps, and then someone pumps your chest to revive life on planet earth. If you are laughing, then you understand me.

Of course, CPR could have another meaning like, "Creation, Promise, Rescue." When you are finally able to put thoughts into speech, the resuscitative effort has been effective. So, don't just jump next time without a good parachute. Winging your way through the elements of friendship can bring on that wonderful world of returning feeling. Never close a door on life, because there is someone out there who will pick up the mangled mess, throw you over his shoulder and run for the emergency room. That holiday which happiness took is over. Now all the joys that are just around the corner are worth the hanging on. And if you are running away from issues, be careful not to smash yourself into the next runner coming from the opposite direction.

For me: A long-distance phone call warmed the day from deep in the winter of Michigan.

CPR with laughing eyes, warm arms and time out for living!

PILLOWS

Punch the pen to the point, and it doesn't matter what anyone thinks, says or does about its line-by-line exercises. As long as these are pillows for comfort, this writer can be propped up or lying down. The pen becomes my long-lost, happy friend. Sometimes I sense its disgust with the rainbow pens waiting in the wings. Its good-old-black ink sinks its purpose into the paper.

Pillows and pens can become best friends amid the stacks of notebooks and literary books of presence.

How freeing the feeling of release to allow the brain to control the pen and keep the tongue silent! Perhaps, words can evoke smiles or tears by forming pictures in a slide show gliding step-by-step across the computer screen.

Indulging in the pillow peacefulness may be the imprint of rest today. Time stops and waits for the writer to rise from the ashes of the past. The pillow understands and never criticizes the awkward expense of hours or minutes. Instead, the pillows exude a fragrance of Japanese pears or lush flower gardens while I prop in the cushiony comfort of the quilt.

There's creative benefit in being comfortable, and writer and reader can either enjoy or ignore the world beyond the curtains of winter. French lace curtains are delicate, and so are the words penning this intent. No lamp needed now - the morning dawn rings its timely rising to announce a new day.

"Hello, out there!" from Pillow Talk.

Phone rings with someone asking for the "Truehearts!" A wrong number, but it honors the expression of truth from the location of a pillow.

SPIRIT OF TRUTH

Starving for a touch and kiss brings wild weather to the emotions of human need. It's the waking in the night or the-never-having-gone to sleep that magnifies this unspoken yearning. The words urge to be spoken, but they are withheld for the sake of civility.

The thought can't be expressed; it is left to be one of life's lacks. This feeling of need is so much like the air we breathe. It can catch us by surprise, as unexpected as a yawn.

Printed words on a page look flat and cold. They could be someone's amusement, but the determination to express may have been forged into steel courage.

Profoundly sensitive is the creative spirit. This tenderness is deeply felt through the long journey from loneliness to the joining of hearts. Bonding can't be measured in growth rings of time. There are invisible moments gifted by intuition that can speed the process. Elusive, intangible love when found is the joy of body, mind, and spirit. It is also the silent laughing for the soul. Moments in time shared in silence, peace and happiness; and woven into the fabric of touch, kiss and prayer. A God-given-blessing to be preserved with care in gratitude.

Amen!

EASY RHYTHM LISTENING

Let nothing separate the rhythms and harmonies of music dancing through the air waves. The composers have transmitted their gifts of notes to set the world moving in a joyous combination of new steps. Listen to "Blueberry Hill," and drift toward the blueberry fields rich in clusters of nature's own. Feel the smoothness of these delicate moments.

Is there an extra-sensory wireless stream of thought hidden from view that transmits a touch of the Maker's own gift?

Explanations are unneeded. It is satisfying enough just to be receiving these unseen waves for hearts to share. An old favorite, "Tara's Theme," brings me to contemplate a painting of Melrose that is quietly sharing my home.

Musical rhythms and lyrics sung transform the page of my day to a lighter turn, as sunshine melts away the icy fingers of winter. What joy when "We've Only Just Begun" is a reminder of the Masters! Let time drift like clouds seen in the blue through the skylight as you feel your own moments of rhythm. It's just Power Steering tapping out a new energy to keep us moving on.

THE TRACE

When disappointment is discovered after the perfect home setting was found, how would you deal? Finding this hand of cards dealt in a casino of homes for sale and the perfect one hidden in a contract, how would you bid?

Reaching for the wheel of editing a manuscript seems to provide the warmth of promise under the spring time sweater.

Someone called, "There's a storm coming! But you are close to the door." The storms of life seem to be so frequent that exposure must be constantly assessed. A two-hundred-year-old pine nods a brief agreement to this thought as it stands against the impending stillness. It's okay, Lord, you are in control, and Power Steering feels only a soft breeze of suggestion.

I pull the sweater collar closer and stay the course of writing through all anxieties. The passages of script can hold a thousand words without ever being a heavy load. And the time spent on a tiny bird's chirping is a heavenly moment recorded. The bird's trills seem to lift the darkening clouds and show light just beyond the next layer. When nature speaks, we can feel its faint vibrancy by being still, silent and peaceful. Springtime softness reigns and souls erase the losses of today. Welcome home is the threshold for tomorrow.

A soft tap of raindrops, like cloud tears touching the evening, refreshes spirit.

DARING

To watch a bungee jumper in a daring leap of faith makes us wonder: Will the heart strings on the cord allow safe descent?

Is this a lesson of life where love is wrapped in hope and faith? The leap isn't down; rather, it is an upward ascent.

The time to make daring risks may take years in the climb. Where are you in your daring journey of living? Are you alone, working toward a plateau in search of a new view?

The view from a lookout point broadens the view of the past beneath the feet and allows the eyes to look to the surrounding heights. If you have never been to the mountains of new adventure, then check your compass and strive toward them. There's joy in the heights. Our astronauts can attest to this glory. The weight of problems is jettisoned behind, and the unknown ahead becomes possible to visit. Daring to find the true life preserver through faith is bundled in your being. Dare to Love! There's the lasting and tangible vehicle of journey!

God gave freedom of choices. The daring to live expansively is yours. The old year has disappeared and the New Year is on the march.

WEARING RED

A strange title, but it surfaced from the past moments of wearing a red jacket. Well, the "Red Coats" of British days in colonial times flaps on a tall museum flag pole to remind me.

However, for this writer, it's a blush at being caught red-handed in the childhood cookie jar. Today, is the day to commemorate an occasion after the Easter season. My jacket is usually worn on Valentine's Day or Christmas. The finger of truth is pointing toward healing from old wounds. There's no band aid to cover the bleeding of words unspoken. The heart pulses powerfully today in a stream of healing prayers sent from inside the red jacket. Thoughts pouring forth of quiet need. I leave the pedal to rest in its standing place on the car floor. Wearing red brings a little chill of memory when a young man from across the ocean of time said, "I don't wear red!" He was such a special young man who sat on a bench for a moment in our town and may today be seated in the center of his own park in an unnamed capital as a statue of hope in an angry world.

I'll always remember this rising student of life. He learned here how to eat an ear of sweet corn with his fingers. Funny, how we wear odd memories so well. Perhaps it's because we are all bonded in this great universe. Red can just be for taking time for stoplights on this road of life. A magic moment of memory!

THE POWER OF "NO!"

The verbal expression of producing the word "No" can be powerful and life-changing. Think about all of the times in your life when this power took over in authority.

It's a negative that can cut deep into the soul and even create a wound that never will heal. It's not the resentment of the word; rather, its influence over fragile creative energy is saddening. The enthusiasm of an idea can be shattered by this force called, "NO!" Throughout life, I have fought off the "NO!", but at times it did become the victor. It's like a pirate breaking through the fog, boarding my ship, and seizing my treasure of joy.

Fighting this foe of "No!" requires the best judgement, critical thinking, and problem-solving skills in the arena. This is a personal enemy. It enters life in the early years, conveyed through the eyes and mind by others.

Stop and think! Imposed discipline can be exercised for good or for bad. "No!" subdues free will. It can destroy the power to choose and the desire to explore. An extroverted child can flee to the safety of withdrawing into self.

We all discipline our pets. There is a need like, "Don't jump on the kitchen table!" Offering alternative ways of being properly fed shows love. So, also, the "No" must be ordered from the menu of good. Not to kill the exuberance of inventions about to become reality is the intention. Our role is to encourage so that ideas bud into fruition. Life thrives when an individual is given gentle loving advice, not threats and obstructions that destroy spirit.

Yes, cover the sneeze that's a germ-breeding burst. There is no vaccination against "No!" to protect creativity. Teaching thinking skills and problem solving are basics that are life-long. Sharing experiences, listening and talking it over are elements of idea building. Impatience closes all the doors.

At this moment, my Persian Kitty entered the open door, and I said, "Hi!" She responded with a "Hmm" purr. She knew the welcome of love, not the cowering of fear. She craves the toenail rub against her fur, and she comes in to purr a "Good night!" It's time to give Tinkerbell a brush in grooming and a feeling of belonging. You see, belonging can be chased away with the harshness of "No!"

Loving and caring words with just the right vocal tone are the guidance instead. Be careful when you use "No!" because its left turns or right turns at red lights are life changing. Little detours with the road signs of guidance can lead to new adventures.

"Thank you Lord, for our sharing time in Power Steering."

DROP BOX

This invisible collection of thoughts just keeps piling up. The combination to place these articles is somewhere out there, and this seems like a race toward fulfillment.

To deny to express the unexpected experience of spirit's touch becomes burdensome if not released. The "drop box" of memories can so easily be misplaced.

A chill, or is it a shivering thrill from a sweeping thought? If there's nothing new under the sun, as an old professor drilled into his students, then has someone else stolen this same moment?

Perhaps the brain has the capacity to accept or reject the instances of time and memory that store in the "drop box." Green lights tell us to roll on through the intersection. Perhaps the drop box is at the bank and secure in its protection. We can't stop dawn from arriving nor hold daylight in our hands. Only God in all His glory can reveal the meaning of the day. What do we store of these instances of time?

"Hello, drop box, let me know your combination. There are no fingerprints on you to show who left these immortal touches."

I have a lifetime of descriptor words from which to make a deposit.

BENEATH THE LINES

Unwritten moments of life missed because, beneath the lines, these couldn't be printed until now. Only from the heart are these events held away from the breaking tears.

Memory focused, but I allowed it to flow away from any obsession of imagination. If you share this in a reading second, then we have met in understanding.

Not a nightmare, just a recognition that the treasure of meeting an artist of world acclaim was lost because there wasn't time to wait overnight for an appointment. An appointment to meet the great Master, Norman Rockwell. To have experienced shaking a hand of history and looking into eyes of the world he saw was so close but was missed by a few hours because no one shared this great desire with me, and I had to go. This cutting loss, recalled from the depths of experiences' hesitation. The release of ache is gone, but the treasure will never be returned. So, beneath the lines of life, there's a sense of wrong, left beside a tombstone somewhere. A shred of marriage buried beneath the lines.

Power Steering has granted peace.

POURING FORTH BLESSINGS

The well, the urn and the cup ready for the greatest source of life to be poured out for all of humanity. The religion of heart is the dedication to put the pen on the foundation and begin to build a strong fortress of strength to carry the weight of purpose.

The mortar is the love ingrained in this tower of thought. Perhaps that is all required to provide the opening of effort: Love.

Good day!!
Good Night!
Skip the "o"
You've spelled God!

DEAR POWER STEERING

Dear Power Steering, I've wondered why you have been so quiet today. There haven't been any intuitive directions, and I feel like I'm in a valley.

Then, suddenly, in this writing moment, I find that you have been occupied with prayers to answer: your focus is to steer Hurricane Erika away from heavy concentrations. I'm sorry! I've been selfish to be tugging on your engine switch operating where and what I should be doing.

You have such a personal touch for each one. All anyone has to do is to open his or her heart to you!

"Thank you, Lord."

LOST

Raindrops and tears are keeping me company. I feel lost in these moments after such a long road on the journey. Suddenly, today, nothing looks familiar, though each possession has bearing of a belonging. I sense inwardly the emotions stirred by each.

Why? Is it the cloudy day of thought and sky? No, it's not depression like a big gaping rut in the road. It's a realization that there's so much to be accomplished, but the where of location is elusive.

I am lost only in feelings and searching for the arms of why. The where is lost, too, in a great big world of choice. The doing is still at the bridge of pen in hand, awaiting the arrival of the navigator.

Found!

Chapter 3: Everyday Life

WHAT IS WORTH?

"Worth," a strangely spelled word that contains a question of "or."

Definitely, self-worth is vital to everyday breathing and success. It's measure of importance is not expressed in monetary denominations; rather, its value is spoken in terms of life, liberty, freedom of speech and peace. Those inherent elements are priceless in the armor of protecting this five letter word, "worth."

If this connects and says enough to you, then the flow of words can ebb to a stop. Because, dear reader of passion and brilliance, your worth is infinitely valuable. Hit the day again, feet on the floor, be it carpet, tile or even the sandy soil of an island, and charge forth in excitement to discover its worth!

TALK

What a pretty little word, *"talk."* It can be a walk of faith in sharing and being vulnerable to deep inner awareness. In the age of smart phones, texting, emails and high tech expression, we sometimes forget to just be eye-to-eye in the talk zone.

I learned to read eyes that talk, way back when I was a kid.

My first strong revelation of how eyes talk came first with animals. Just like Dr. Doolittle. My beautiful, huge, black, Newfoundland dog, Lassie, had wonderfully expressive eyes. I watched her, and I could tell when she was happy or sad. I didn't know this just from the wag of her tail. Her eating my summer straw hat and the look in her eyes told me that she was a fun lover.

Oh, yes, on a big Midwest farm, there were all kinds of animals, and the baby calf became a pet. She grew and grew and grew and became a big Angus cow. When it was dinner time, if the "help" didn't get out to feed the herd, she would announce her presence at the big old Victorian house with a moo, maybe, or by getting up on the porch to nudge the back entrance door. She had the most gorgeous brown eyes that I loved to discern. She didn't show terror, like I did, when she fell through the cellar door. I screamed in panic, "Blackie fell through the cellar door, and she's in the basement!" Instead, she just climbed back up the steps as if she had innate knowledge how to get out of trouble. This episode wasn't mirthful until later.

To me, as a kid, the chickens' eyes were kinda' strange: One eye was on one side of the head and the other was on the other side. That made those eyes hard to read! So, I just cuddled the chicks, which resulted in my having to get at least five clean dresses from the clothesline each day. Sometimes things get out of hand.

So, back to the reading of eyes for happiness or sadness during the newness of meeting a person: Look deep and read. There's much non-vocalized verbiage coming from eyes, and without discernment, the messages are hidden from the giver and the receiver.

Discernment is a natural gift or a learned skill. When no words vocalize what is stirring in the heart, the words of the eyes express the mystery within. Try this gentle art of communication, and it will bring a new understanding of God's great humanity!

And the animal kingdom as well!

MEANT TO BE!

When some are going to bed and others are going to work, there's a semblance of feeling that everything is in balance. Awake or asleep, the world feeds on progress. It takes all kinds of effort to maintain the earthly spin of rhythm. Whether the efforts are low or high in energy, each person revitalizes the breathing world.

Put the cap on the pen, rub the eyes of sleepiness, and find stress-free moments to realize that the power of heaven is in charge.

Power steering may be silently waiting for another moment caught on the edge of time to bring joy. Following the lanes along the way, it does all good in its smoothing purpose. "Hello" to wakefulness and gratefulness that the Higher Power gently guides thought into action! The momentum is in proportion to its progressive speed. We can put the gear shift in park or reverse, or we can select drive and begin to accelerate to change the road map of course.

When that choice is made, the gear of drive rolls us through gliding times of sight, sound and elation!

Choice is a blessing!

ASSIGNMENTS

The assignments undertaken in the school of learning can be completed with ease or merged onto the shelves of research.

The unseen urge to continue writing feels like an assignment from a power beyond self. It is a mystery not to be left unsolved.

Perhaps only nudging these words onto the page for light is all that's required. Is there a silent demand from beyond time and space to be formed into words?

Pollen can be an allergy nuisance, but the glory of being the instrument, however allergic, to receive a divine assignment is awesome. Could it be the angels of time reaching out to whomever is awake and available to record? Savor and swallow the gulping instant of surprise. The assignments allow hearts to explore great depths in the search for discovery. My sharing this with you today occurs before tiny dewdrops glistening in the morning sun melt into the soil of life. We are instruments of heaven's earthly wanderers. To them we appear like little vagabonds searching for knowledge. For us, the assignment arrives without a lecture and is placed for viewing in this great arena called time.

This author wanted to use the word "life" in that sentence, but "time" moves far beyond.

LESSONS LEARNED

Profoundness sticks in the throat not only as words, but also as deeds. It can be when the intuitive springs forth a title, but, in an instant, that disappears with the ticks of the clock. It happened to me yesterday when a schedule took front seat and the writing dejectedly climbed into the back seat. So what do you think? Me too. The lesson to learn is now a day gone.

We engage in so many lists of appointments that the vital link to hidden expression is also in that company keeping.

To become engaged passionately in the purpose which we have been given is a bell ringing in distant thought. How loud it chimes may only peal in memory. This ringing chime is a reminder to be fruitful and not be a slave to routine and schedule.

A stack of clothing catalogs does not have even a trace of lure for me today. The lesson learned is to be alive and mindful of the sensitivities that surround the needs of others. For some I am feeling the lesson of visualizing, and for others, I draw upon the deep inner well of impressions of them.

Waiting and doing sit on the balance scales, while the hand of need points to choice. The gift of intuition is a miracle in living lessons. Braided into our busy lives, this gift is like the colorful light from a new morning after cloudy days.

Shining rays through new born oaks leaves are a reminder of beauty in being at the right window of the season. Lessons learned! The bell is tolling. The class is completed. Credit received is the merit of having attended.

"Thank you, Lord!"

THE LIGHT

There's a light that shines in the day and night. It's likened to a lighthouse on the shore to keep safety in view. This light is stronger than the electric lamp just now turned on. It is the light of prayers that form a network shining throughout the universe.

Strong and powerful, this light doesn't extinguish. It's a beacon radiance that shines through the eyes of all.

The Light is the Spirit of Truth and Honor: A haven of strength that should not be snuffed out by unacceptance.

Not taking time to light our beacons is to reject wisdom. We must be a source. Shining the light is the duty of each in a world where darkness wants to be victor. Shine forth, oh light of day and night, through storms of fire, wind and water that ply all situations!

Let this light be the beacon that grows brighter and stronger through time, a guiding force of safety.

Yes, I write this now, but not without denying this time of edging sleep into a coverlet, beneath the heart of love. Truth is lived every day. Truth is a light of power and glory for the ages of man.

My eyes are closing, but someone else is waking to work in the storehouse of shining fruitfulness.

There's no roar in this soaring Grace. It is Light burning brighter. Like a song with lyrics, "I Can See Clearly Now"!

(I set down the pen and paper as the purring kitty comes to keep me company in soft-stroking contentment.)

HUMMINGBIRD OF PURPOSE

The morning light has brought a hummingbird in flight. It resembles a tiny leaf in fluttering motion. A thought just as delicate as the nectar that this little giant of the winds needs for survival. The wings of time fly equally by and must be preserved, not in a shopping bag of great expanse, but in the leaves of a book to share for all of mankind. We're on our way into the heavens of finding truth, light and love.

Never have these keys rung so much energy that it out-flies the fountain pen of yesterday. Where are we going? Only truth and love can answer any question of the moment.

I've never looked up from this little entrancing keyboard tonight. I am sure that I will find the keys have caught what no net of expression can hold.

Seconds recorded but never felt as they dissolved. A surprise that 147 words and counting have been so brief! What records do we all leave from the moment of NOW? Footsteps in muddy delight at pictures to preserve or hosiery that has worn out toes? Nothing as beautiful as feelings that are absorbed as the heart fills with wonder, joy and warmth. Try It! Share!

CROSSING OVER

Crossing over doesn't have to be like the toothpaste that collects into a big glob at the end of the tube. No, think about how you brush your teeth: from left to right, up and down, and then you floss between. That's an everyday thing, usually after several meals and especially after desserts. "Yum!"

Now, Left and Right are as easy to understand as brushing your teeth. Left brush of the organizational hemisphere of the brain. Right brush for the creative side. "YUP!" This is persuading, or you may say, "Get out of my face." I'll laugh and say, "You just wait for the clean feeling!"

I'm in a big hurry, but stopping and doing the most important becomes the "left" in prioritizing. I jump from the shower, grab the tooth brush, organize my thoughts while brushing, and then write the absurdity on paper that you will read.

My computer wasn't connected to the internet yet. So this little beginning is born out of a key in sharing. The bare bones in doing the most important! Now if you are on my thinking train or just waiting beside the rails that's okay. ALL ABOARD! We're about to unlock, "Focus and success."

Hi, Social Media! I just figured out how to arrange my continental love of teaching and talking to all my elementary children across the years.

Oh, did I derail? Sorry! Laugh! Let's get on to the next station and figure out left and right and straight ahead in combinations that create less work and worry. Crossing over to the median: Make your work and thought lists.

Headings:
LEFT – ORGANIZATION
RIGHT – CREATIVE
COMBINING: MEETS IN THE MEDIAN.
Make your lists under each, and then check off the items as you accomplish them. Afterward, reward yourself with something enjoyable, perhaps e-mail, a phone call, or just a comfort zone chair.

LET'S PRETEND

When radio was queen of the airwaves, there was a program in the late afternoon called, "Let's Pretend".

Perhaps this was the access to creative thinking introduced to kids sitting in a big arm chair by the heating pipes. Oh, it was a comfy, warm setting that might almost put anyone into a snoozing mode. Maybe that was a parent's own little quiet time.

This program held stories of make-believe in far off places and under starlight dreams. A melodic voice weaved the story web enchantingly as music played in the background. The exercises of imagination became a longed-for afternoon treat. It didn't take candy bribes to just sit still and learn to listen. These were the kid moments which became the movie events of the mind to propel the child into a vast universe of pretense. Playing dress up with high-heel shoes thanks to the magic of playroom time. So "Let's Pretend" birthed a plethora of heroes, heroines and helpful animal characters.

Do you remember what sent you into a realm of creative thinking in your childhood days? The passion of writing, reading and listening became a lifeline of purpose throughout this author's life. So, *let's pretend* that we have met and indulge ourselves in the joys of life together.

CHILLS

Do you have a chill? Check the thermometer, and it could be room temperature, body temperature, or just plain emotion leaving a mark as it passes by.

I had a chilly shiver, and I was ready to climb under the beckoning nighttime quilt. Then a warming thought like a blanket of dreams fell over me and calmed my chill of enlightenment. Quivers can be little body vibrations speaking the silent language of moving on.

Here comes another chill just after a warming thought: the youthful call of, "Chill Out!" Oh, it can have a version of interpretation. So grab a Kleenex. It may be a cold uninvited or an allergy trying to convey extra evidence of an unwanted visitation. Lozenge out the cough if it begins to erupt into the audible.

Or chills can be the nudge of the Great Creator ready to advise, like the nurse practitioner who will explain the meaning of symptoms. Have no fear, if these chills bring goose bumps of surprise. Dare to face your own chilling moments that inevitably appear when one lives fully. Skip the paper clips and sticky notes, and be ready to discover the "GOOD" in daring.

KEEPING ON

The pages of time turning forward. Weathering of lines reaching out to speak. Direction of purpose powered by this heartbeat of pounding joy. Penning the design intended to tune senses - a great surprise for the ones who can let go! "Keeping on" reveals the hidden gifts of perseverance.

Each one of us is a human work of art giving the world insights to the beyond.

How our plan of purpose and our path to destiny are encrypted in wireless messages within us!

Sensitivity to self and others is the key to these turning pages of soul growth. Feelings of grace have no time line in arriving or departing.

Just keep on with the hand of willingness to share. Perhaps sharing is the most purposeful skill to acquire on earth's journey. Keeping On is a challenge in each day to re-create the world in lighter, brighter and more beautiful colors.

EXCAVATIONS

Drilling deep into the well of being requires a powerful drill, because self-defense mechanisms resist, saying, "Not me!"

The Higher Power is gentle in letting the intuitive strengthen so that the excavation can begin. It has to power down through the tough scars of negative experiences and rinse those away. Deeper still lie the hidden tunnels of fear, but the power steering of the drill lightens the load on the drive shaft. Suddenly, the treasure is revealed: the inner gold which has been preserved for your discovery since before time began.

The excavation of your reality ends in recognizing your self-worth and the life-springs of your vitality.

I'll try it with you. I was in the claustrophobia of an old elevator caught between first and second floor. My welling of fear was diminished by an old historian who gave a lesson in Mississippi lore and a Philadelphia story. The layer of claustrophobia disappeared as I relaxed and realized what had hidden within me. It had dissipated thanks to the man's gentle stories that enabled me to release my fear. This was an easy excavation that renewed my strength.

What might be one of your disabling fears?

HIDEAWAY

Just off the heavy duty highways of life here in Virginia is a perfect hideaway-eatery. Order a Billy Mitchell sandwich, a huge delight so big you need to share. Savor the ranch dressing that drenches turkey, ham, cheese and lettuce with a mystery of seasoning.

While we are here with views of the runway, let's imagine chartering a brand new helicopter to take a historic view of our Colonial America. Breathtaking and awesome, and on our return we can celebrate with Bumbleberry pie!

Placemat history reveals that Virginia has provided eight Presidents who have covered the supervision of 42,777 square miles and currently 8.3 million Virginia residents. If you are new in joining us, add one more. No one wants to leave this mecca called, "Virginia Is for Lovers."

Special Note: Outside my luncheon, the new big black helicopter is currently assessed by my "guesstimation" as a property of Home Land Security. Sure a good feeling watching the pilots check out their awesome charge!

THE POWHATAN LAKE REFLECTION

The giant ball of moon pouring beams upon the lake and bringing echoes of light is a touch of heaven meeting planet earth. The moment's illuminated wisdom gets captured by the eye of the owner's camera. He brings the brilliance of the evening into focus. His gentle touch of camera shutter is held in deep reflection by this builder of light and happiness.

A SURPRISE VOCABULARY

There's a little two letter word that seems to be a baby dinosaur of past extinction. However, recently it was a privilege to see a large stone dinosaur egg, not in a museum, but in a rare collection in a private home.

This little two letter word could be a great find to be placed back into everyday vocabulary. It holds so much of what our world needs in creating togetherness and bonds of strength. It's not an anchor word or an expression to fear to use. Instead, it's a bond of friendship. It can hold love in tiny expression. Are you trying to figure out this wordsmith's miracle of untiring devotion to building speech awareness?

There's an even smaller word that can play a game at a party. Giving each party-goer five toothpicks, you can bestow a treasure's worth of sticks. For every conversation with others, when this little word is used, they must give up a toothpick. This little time for icebreaking can be fifteen minutes of conversation. The winner is proclaimed, "Best Winning Friend."

Oh, we forgot to mention the two letter word!

It's the rich expression in life to share: "WE!" The "we" means belonging.

The smaller game changer is, "I" How often we speak more of self as the ego prompts. So try "we," giving "I" a little more silence in the revelation of who you are. We can all be gentler, kinder and more loving people.

"Hello World!"

And we can be best in saying, "I Love You!" If you use the "I" word, use it to tell someone, "I Love You!"

GONE

Why should "gone" be such a powerful word engine for change? Think about the opportunities that weren't considered and which disappeared behind the curtain of "Gone!"

It is a heavy word that can reek with loss, a legacy that is never a productive and positive outcome. No need for regrets because "Gone" can't be erased, but it can be the motivator not to turn your back on even little things. Like leaving the plants un-watered, and suddenly the sun has withered these gentle little creations.

Now little "undones" can become the "dones" of determination. Giving a family member an unexpected, "Thank you", at the front door or car door, for example! "Thank you" can be a powerful steering force in building and mending relationships. The hug of appreciation conveys your inner feelings.

"If only" becomes "I did," "I can," I will." These are the foundations of happiness unwrapped and shared. "Gone" just lost its power, and now you are in charge, a big generator for greatness. Live like an artist painting your own Masterpiece. Try to imagine how God will feel when you have found your personal worth and purpose.

JOY! JOY! JOY!

Simple sounds can turn the ignition key to memories and allow Power Steering to change the course of the day. Stop and wait in the quiet of Now and notice the surrounding sounds that fill the air waves with energy. Just the accomplishment of turning on the washing machine and listening to the water fill the basin does a great job with its cycling assignment. Ordinary sounds can be stimulating. I hear the recycling truck stopping out front. My household contributions are ready for another assignment.

Perhaps recycling sounds will bring a rainforest of the Northwest with the sounds of waterfalls just out of earshot. Simple sounds can bring back a visual holiday of surf rolling against the sand. And subsequently, the spellbinding surprise after a raging storm to find little wooden pieces of a shipwreck from the eighteenth century.

Sounds bring gifts of refreshment, and these are your very own treasures of the moment of now.

The laughing of a child or the soft purr of a kitty. The gentleness of your listening spirit awakens memories and revelations.

Go and discover your private sounds of joy and freedom where your body, mind and soul join in a chorus of timeless joy.

WALKING SOCIOLOGY

To be a sociologist is achievable every day. Everyone is a walking book, carrying the DNA that forms them into a social and cultural work of art.

The grocery store is a great place to find magnificent encounters with individuals. I had a fascination with the apparel of a lady, white scarf wound around her head and framing a beautiful face without makeup. To study her face and watch her behavior was a delight, and I was determined that she would look at me and see me smiling at her. You see, the young cashier had a look of disdain on his face, and it didn't need to be shared. In watching her behavior, I saw that she knew how to use a cream-colored credit card and push the buttons of the scanner expeditiously. The distance precluded seeing which cultural bank icon adorned the card.

Finally, she looked at me as I was smiling. Her face showed an expression of surprise, maybe a little shock, and I would have loved to have heard her speak. For me, her reaction was a sociology class on the move.

Hello World, we live in a wonderful small town for growing up.

The local newspaper, Saturday edition, was the fascination of the cashier as he read the front page which I had just purchased. It made me wonder if perhaps his journalistic encounters normally came from other sources. Just maybe we can guess that his news resources are in video form from the televised media or internet. Small observations of people's behaviors lead us into the wonder of their stories. Awareness is what makes us notice. It is a practiced skill. To share that I always wanted to be a sociologist and was told, "No, that's not in our curriculum. Being a teacher is what we best do." So I'm lucky to have had the set of energies that have given me the privilege to discern lives from an awareness that allows me to share my love for people.

"I love people!"

SATURDAY ROLLERS

It's awfully hard to be both a "Hopeless Romantic" and an author who forgets correct punctuation.

The hair dryer sends a cool blast of air. Changing to "high" setting could result in another surprise! Up on high brings a surge of turning the clock back to other moments. Just "Sweet Dreams" the night before sent me to a deep peace in which drifted the nighttime hours.

This day of color is sparkling in the sunshine outside. The proprietor stirs a brush of color. She's sweeping hair strands of a realtor into a poster-advertising award. Oh, well, that's a long shot or short sale, but the realtor will be a walking model soon. They nod in serious delight at the results, and that beauty shop appointment with a life make-over has been fun to observe. What shade are your colorful choices? Do they enchant the colors of our eyes? Power Steering is a happy companion, whether listening to life stories or easing the glide of a pen writing.

Brown heavy shoes with sturdy shoe strings. Hands folded, fingers crossed, the gentleman lowers his chin to expose a square cut. He's enjoying a shampoo luxury before a trip to the Outer Banks... I'm guessing just for fun. It's great to see men indulging in moments of car keys in the pocket and relaxed smiles. This time is needed as much as the basketball player's shot for the three-pointer! Freedom! Let the clock sweep on and life flow. Both genders can seek hamlets of frozen time and forgotten weather forecasts. If you can't see the benefits of little time outs, then put on your glasses.

He's getting a haircut while the lady for a manicure is being patient. "Saturday rollers" is my time for enjoyment, too!

POWER STEERING 2

When Power Steering 2 bursts onto the printed line, it will have to include little inside events.

Getting ready for a big Chesapeake Bay Writers Gala, the November luncheon, this author had to get up early this morning. To laugh is such a release of emotions, and having my dress properly zipped in back meant just that. So my daughter could zip me in before her busy day. Otherwise, my bursting at the seams in a new dress would spell disaster! Kinda' like the vacuum sucking up my summer dress into the distress zone at the self-serve car wash by the cleaning hose. See, writers can hide embarrassment between the lines and skip the blushing. Almost!

THE EDGE

The edge of day awakens to a new Thanksgiving. The edge brings awareness that the mind and soul work together for amazing discovery. The wireless and digital connect a witness to a New Age bringing rare enlightenment into the miracle of God's love.

We have walls separating physical togetherness. The climb of years can span it. The separated hold on to hope. Faith and love are rungs on the ladder that sets against the walls of life. Questioning begins the quest, prompted by late sunrise slow to scale a wall of mountainous height.

Can faith, love and age bridge the wall of separation? Only time will answer. Having patience, venturing into the unknown and claiming peace may achieve the bonding. The edge holds no fear of heights. This new day dawns with brilliance. What shining moment will it reveal? A Thanksgiving in which God holds the prize-winning ticket for you?

There is no lottery. The edge of new day arrived due to time and purpose united.

Are youth and age bonding on the brink? Golden sands, and oceans rising. Life's eternal gift.

Matching jackets and pants for everyday wear, or life jackets for the storms?

ALIVE

Trusting the intuitive can feel as precarious as walking a high tightrope with no net beneath. The heights can't be measured by the eyes or a prayer gauge, but by the exhilaration when the terminal platform is filled with relief and joy!

Each person has their own experiences of this sensitivity. This afternoon, after errands, lunch and a power-builder 30-minute nap, I was going on another little adventure. Suddenly, I got very ill, almost dizzy, with no explanation except some rushing business in the kitchen. Then the phone rang, and it was my dear friend calling across the wired waves from Florida. By sitting on the stair steps and sharing book ideas and new adventures with her, I vanquished my upset stomach! It wasn't just the calming of nerves. It was also obeying the intuitive charge of "stay at home." And there we were in stair-step conversation. All this writer can say is that the "Great Protector" does look after us.

Earlier this morning, I was ready to make a right-hand turn to the beauty shop, and an unobserved truck crossed my path. He was pulling a very long wagon for hauling debris. No problem, because the brakes were quick to react! I said, "Thank you, Lord."

As I do now! It's the everyday that keeps us on our toes, bringing us to awareness of Higher Power, self and surroundings.

LENS IN FOCUS

Cameras, all sizes and features, require the lens to be in focus for a beautiful clear picture. However, the lens of the human eye just might be too hurried to take in the wholeness of the object.

After years of picking up and admiring a little Anna Lee mouse on my table, I had never really seen the details in this fun little collectible. The jaunty green cap on a little tilted mouse head, its bright eyes, and its face smiling something serious or not certain. There was the mouse hand holding the artist brush poised to begin work, but I never had taken in the armload of colors for choice. They had been there all the time. Strange, how we just might be like one who sees the mouse ready to paint but does not fully see the talent! The mystery of why we don't see fully isn't explained by the absence of eyeglasses but by the hurry of the eye to see another object.

Is this also true of the ones around us, whom we never really get to know deeper than a surface handshake?

I always focus on the eyes of the people I meet, and I listen as their eyes speak. Their clothing is not so important, for these are so changeable. The eyes are the unique identifiers of the individual. The eyes themselves never change, but arched eyebrows, laughing or crying bespeak many changes.

Even in passing of years, I remember the eyes of former students whose names may now elude me. The eyes are doorways behind which are rooms full of magnificent gifts. Appreciating the miracles within comes from awareness steered from sensitivities that we may develop. Perhaps my former students remember me because I shared this as their teacher. What a wonderful world of memories for all of us!

Today, I'll just take off my guilty surprise at the little creative mouse and move him to a more visible position of appreciation.

SATURDAY

The morning isn't early, it's just the usual hands of the clock ticking out a good idea to wake up.

In quiet before the family wakes, cats, too, are still curled up and snug. The thought of the day's schedule is simple, but to wrap my brain around all the writing words makes me want to choose which ones to postpone into the future and which ones are in the *now*.

It's almost like a "Shake & Bake" mix. It doesn't have the King Arthur's label or the posted expiration date. The word, "date," was hurriedly scribbled and became spelled, "late." Perhaps this is Power Steering slipping in some fun and amusement! Many ask, "Are you sure you're having fun?" And why is this a concern in a tired world? "OOPS!" This word without an underline had never crossed the dark line before. I believe in sunshine and not past shadows.

Postage stamps are standing up and waving in the calling of "To do!" So, first, send a book to a resident with wavering health in a big care-warehouse filled with hungry, anxious people needing outside love. Whew, that's a tough expression of a system trying to heal and entertain its residents, who measure their days with the prescription bottles labeled "good for refills" or "no refills!"

"Hey, Lord, no disrespect, but this hadn't even crossed the brain cells of my mind until now. Are you sure I got it right?"

Now the Persian kitty wanting to be fed knocks at my bedroom door. Lord, I love how you feed us daily with the manna of work and happiness. What a joy, the marvels of miracles that can stop negative attacks and give insight to awaken a world of closed eyes hiding from reality with *pills*!

Stop! It's time to address the envelope and tuck *Time on the Turn* snuggly into the envelope. I just got a chill that my warm, old purple bathrobe cannot conceal. Was profundity infused into this day, I wonder? Only I can know, and, yes, the purple pen also.

A little hush of silence closes this page. Thank you, Lord, for your Power Steering presence. Good gracious, I just ran out of books to gift and stationery for personal notes, too. Time for another refill order which is overdue, maybe today!

INVISIBLE GREEN LIGHT

One of my former students from classroom days just gave me the best gift. Sarah said, "Oh, I loved your book, *Time on the Turn*, and my Mom is reading it now. We're passing it around." This gift of words was responded with my giving her a big hug of gratitude. Yes, the invisible green light became visible. Thank you, Lord, when the brake lights were about to pull over for all other book store authors racing through the narrow aisles and the world of books. I'll just keep gifting and forget to ask for shelf space. I like the personal encounters that are dramatic and meaningful. This is the royalty of my success, just for your children, Lord.

IT'S MOTHERS DAY

OH MY! Catch a fleeting thought and put it in the jewelry box. The gifts of children in sharing with Mom.

A long time ago, when life was new and traditions were passed along, at church on Mother's Day, there were people wearing pink or white carnations. So pins were distributed according to the answer of the question, "Living or gone?" To a child's ears, what did that mean? Out came one, and my Mother was given a white one, and my sister and I were given pink. In my childish curiosity, I didn't want my Mother to have a white one when she was so lovely wearing pink. She never knew my little wish, and, today, I must wear white.

The alarm just went off in a shrill announcement that sleep time is over. It's Mother's Day, and in hours the family arrives for a dinner menu of extraordinary preparation by one son-in-law of "Chef" acclaim in our family. Suddenly, the beautiful table is highlighted with a dozen roses.

"Thank you, family."

I'll just add happy thoughts to the bouquets of pink and white carnations worn in memory. Traditions seem to just quietly ebb away, and perhaps recording this will be lost too. Then my other son-in-law shared that back somewhere in the 50's or before, baby boys were given pink ribbons in the nursery and baby girls were to wear blue ribbons. It's true that pink is the stronger color and blue is gentle. Why was it changed, blue for pink, for a gender distinction?

Mother's Day and Father's Day are every day, so there is no need to celebrate only once a year. A family is the greatest gift of everyday. Skip the pink and white carnations, and leave those beauties for someone's other commemorative bouquet.

I always have loved the word, "bouquet." It has such a pretty shape in thought. It can dance right out of a garden, nursery grower's skill, or a florist's talent. Worn with joy, and today it has brought Mother's Day pride.

"Hi, family, with love!"

(Read in the cozy, warm kitchen filled with aromas, hugs, smiles and love.)

Chapter 4: The Sensory Power

THE POWER OF TOUCH

The power of touch is unexpected, light, but strong; and its impression is similar to raindrops on the skylight which run away in an instant, like a yawn without any remnant remaining. The delicate awakening of senses might disappear faster than reaching for the note pad to record its feelings and stimulations.

A touching memory drifts to a saw mill and a downstream eddy. The contents of a small and touching gift box might be enormously potent, but the elemental content is the moment of reminding others that you care. Wrapping love inside a touch with a beautiful ribbon of praise may be life support to a hurting person.

Touch is a miracle that can heal with a little shot of electrical stimulation, a CPR that revitalizes the moment. At times, we associate "touch" with an ecstasy building from anticipation. The degree can't be measured; it's a gift of expression light and powerful that scales fail to register. Its rhythm lulls to rest the soul in need of renewal. The heart is primed to pump a deep well of encouragement as nourishing as artesian water. Physical touch can drive away despair hidden in the cells of life. It energizes a jump into a new direction. It's like Mother's Day, a birth of life.

Senses become visible through the chiffon covering the soul of life. They lie under the tangible of the clothing moment, where the power of touch blends with the awareness of light. Where this gift originates is in the seed of the Master's touch, planted and awaiting the watering of hope and soon sprouting to the visible. The chiffon is a curtain lightly veiling the air of awareness underneath. It casts no shadow upon the heart of healing.

An author can't write the recipe behind touch. He or she can only share that this keen sensitivity is a treasure from the all Higher Power. It is real and universally felt. The reader closes the page in wonder of his individual encounters. Breathless in surprise, both author and reader receive, without asking, new insight.

Intuitive, you have touched again this time unmeasured by a clock as it spins on! Seconds of praise! The Power of Touch! Just like lighting a candle and feeling its glow!

Now I have an empty pen, ready for refilling. I see on my page an old-fashioned touch of happiness that we all are the beneficiaries of God's great expression.

Thank you, Lord, for these pillars of strength and power. Touch holds a miracle. It's yours to discover! Watch and sense the instant in time. Nestle down and rest, ready for another encounter with the Power of Steering.

LITTLE VOICE

When you are writing a book, you feel like living right inside the heart beating time. It seems to penetrate the deeper core of thinking, feeling and wholeness. To question this effort is everyone's right, but there's no question as to the power of discovering inspiration. A divine ladder climbing into the heavens of the Maker of All Creation, at heights above the atmospheric jet streams flowing west to east and beyond to the breathless reaches of the stars.

The guided hand of the pen overcomes the arthritis of clumsiness with the looseness of flowing in hot wax. It is effortless. It's not a feeling of rapture; rather, a genuine hope for providing peace on the very physical level of here and now.

Just a little voice of encouragement can ignite the engine of Power Steering and jumpstart new momentum. When throwing back the quilt to turn off the light, I find the compelling force to first express the love and joy of today, learning and recognizing.

Thank you, God. Receive my prayers for precious family and friends, whose true needs are only known to you above. We all live under the canopy of the sky blue that changes with the cloud formations. We all live on the same planet, and this means we're close and never far away.

GUARDIAN

"Dear Lord, I have to take one step at a time. Help me to do this step by step toward a new goal you have in sight. It's a peaceful reminder that you are in charge, but with the free will you've given, I hope it's the choice you would approve."

We always seem to be living on the edge of new adventures, and when the glowing green lights are ready, I always think and say, "Thank you, Lord." One day, you lit my way through all green stoplights, but at the last one, you shone an amber glow of caution. I became alert to the next intersection of choice. Did I make the one you had in mind?

Intimate sharing with you is like slowly unpacking a heavy load. In some cultures, loads are baskets carried on heads, and, in others, yokes around necks. But the immeasurable weight that the brain circuits carry can be heavier. Gradually, we can unravel these binding thought waves with fingers of quiet contemplation and prayer. There is a joy of sharing with you, Lord, and I sense often the unseen presence of our guardian-angel friends.

ANCHORING

What do you think of when you see or contemplate an anchor? This morning, holding my cup, I reflect that no one has named a coffee brand to honor the word, "anchor." A coffee so named could accompany our voyage later.

Anchor drops through the rhythmic waves rocking a ship that pauses in a safe haven. From a steady point, we make choices of how long to remain or what might be the next port of call. It gives us a new starting point to venture from our temporary home to new places in the local surroundings. Perhaps we make small excursions in a little skiff, a canoe, or a motor boat. If we stop and deep-breathe right now, it feels for this moment that we may be anchored and ready to visit the tropical island's beauty. Oceans of thoughts and islands of wonder!

There are other kinds of anchors, like a home purchased where roots of the surrounding environment feel welcoming and the hospitality of local natives warms the air. We bask in the solace of belonging. A family is built on this anchor of protection. It promises a place for safe return from ventures to work or excursions into new experiences. Family becomes a haven slowly and intricately constructed in our little harbors. Each one within the family can feel the power of steering from the ship's bridge. You are the captain of your destination, but always there's the anchor's steadiness upon returning.

Anchors may be persons, places or things. Even a website can provide an anchorage to the world beyond its pages! Expressions and feelings reach out, and, suddenly, you are an anchor to someone.

Do you have an anchor? Or are you still sailing the seas in search of this element? Could the harbor of God's promises be the store settlement for ship supplies, compass and anchor?

I leave you these thought-pictures for you to envision your own harbor of happiness. There you will find no turbulence when you drop anchor. In the feeling of security, you can experience joy. Map your own paths and returns.

You have a new beginning! Hold on!

REACHING

Finding nothing in a reach for time could be a moment of rare purity. Thoughts flow without recording and remain within the heart. Is this love or the essence of life caught in a little sigh?

Reaching for an object, I find it may be become nothing important. Is this Spirit within training me to listen to silence? Answers to unexpressed questions seem to flow from pen tip on to the day sometimes. I feel like I am floating in a gentle stream above soft green moss. I pass nodding, wild violets and emerge to a pastoral view of perfection. Ahead, I see that I will pass under a bridge. Is this the elusive bridge between the spirit of thought and the hard core of language?

Reaching for elements invented in the wireless age of messages from sender to receiver: This can be a touch of heavenly plan to experience but not truly to understand.

The power of steering thoughts from the mist of a darkened world to steady eternal light opens a new page for living. We find a breathless presence. Without touching, we know it exists: The Holy Spirit so delicately observed in the light that a ragged, random thought can send it away. Harshness is not permitted in the upper world of time. Powerful, unseen and yet existing, the Presence requires us to erase restlessness. Only then is the source of the light found.

Walking barefoot into this new space evokes stratospheric feelings. A little itch of the shoulder may well be the touch of angel wings brushing past. Surprise gives birth to wonderment. If we allow our journey of seconds to visit, we remain with joy trimmed and tied on a plate of happiness.

We glance at the clock. It has no face. Time has flowed to eternity.

CONTENTMENT 2

I see her walking my way. I discern the shape of contentment in her radiant smile. Her facial expression bestows gifts upon person after person as she walks throughout her day. Her smile is a mini-oasis in a world of populating deserts.

Rooted in natural strength, branches of contentment extend to shade and shelter friendships. Contentment is not something purchased across the counter. It's a God-given pleasure. Sometimes it arrives as a consequence of achieving goals. Such satisfaction! Feeling this inner peace frees us from our ropes of tension.

We draw strength from each sharing of contentment. Witnessing others holding hands or entwining arms in the rushing world may be a reminder to us of missing links. When we experience the joy of contentment, even seconds become eternal as we remember forever this treasure of moments in time.

Pursue the goal of discerning truth in things as small and light as a smile. Take the silent path of listening, observing and accepting. Congratulations on your journey's start. You are not required to carry a paper map.

"Thank you, Lord."

AN INTERLUDE

The call of an owl awakens the forest day, even before the sun has caught its rays on the Eastern Shore. In the quiet between its calls, there is assurance that all is well! The hurricane of violence in the Caribbean has been torn apart by the blessed mountain peaks out there. Islands that flooded fears are now still standing on their volcanic foundations from eons of creeping lava and spewed ash. The features of palms remain symbols to remind us of warmth and beauty still remaining.

Dear little owl, somewhere out there, you are quiet now. Your sleepy little eyes foretell a day of safety.

Prayer to higher power brings photo focus to Power Steering. Time is zooming in, and visual sensitivity too is returning. No windshield wipers today! The morning shoreline is free of fog. Pilots of ships map their directions on calming seas.

YOU NEVER KNOW

You never know when life's little surprises will emerge. Sometimes, when the pen is set aside and thought is put to rest, the unexpected sneeze breaks the silence. The pen drops to the floor and demands its retrieval. If a sneeze is heart-stopping, then how can we deal with the unexpected? The unexpected may be a situation of either thrive or survive. You never know what miracle is caught in a wave or embrace of greeting. But daily we walk towards unforeseen chances.

To stand in a median and let the world go by, never noticing the muddy road, costs us opportunity. We miss things. You never know that a soul-meeting-soul happened in a most unusual place, a parking lot of filled spaces. So chuckle at the "You never know", and alert your senses to the universe of surprises. "Unaware" becomes the challenge of igniting "awareness" that our guardian angel, or a whole fleet of angels, have lit the road leading to our destinies.

Leave the muddy shoe marks to wash into the soil. Mist and raindrops, as soft as a kitten's nudge, sound gently on the window, while, in the distance, a cupboard door closes.

You never know what treasured memory waits behind the doors of the heart.

TONES

Train your ears to the tones surrounding every day. This dimension speaks another unwritten language.

Start first with listening to the articulation of a special individual, and you'll soon recognize this person by voice rather than face. It's an identifying vocal signature of authenticity. Then begin to listen for his modulation, which conveys spectacular emotions, invisible to the eyes, but, to the ears, a unique harmony.

We think of tones being in the musical gallery, and this is ever true. A beat of a drum and tinkling of chimes sound their tones.

The vocal train has a personal track that can be warming, chilling or alarming. Listen carefully to tones of a person. And if you can, watch the tonal kinesics of body language. There is a mystery in the awareness that arrives to us, and it's not in a textbook for a test question. The inner being tunes to life's generous messages and communications.

Power Steering, you drive along amazing avenues and freeways of expression.

The best is the avenue of, "I love you!"

HART'S MANSION

In the presence of silence, there's treasure of moments. Take time to allow the thinking cells of creativity to become connected. Little seconds grow into fine-tuned minutes in the midst of silence that makes time both fleeting and eternal.

My sensitivity is sharpened. The hands of time release new feelings from the vacuum of the past. I find leisure that allows pleasure to come into focus. My personal camera lens captures the light radiance.

Today I went on a search for an old-fashioned mansion that I loved many years ago. My ancient photograph captures the experience of that old house in hues of strong pillars of history. There's a spirit of love that still surrounds this very old remnant I see today. The trees hold sway to the seasons of the past. For me, the day became an adventure across the great James River through springtime countryside to the mansion preserved again for new memories.

FLASH LIGHT, PLEASE

"Lights out, curfew today," is proclaimed by my body which sprints towards, "Good night.". Head on the pillow, but out pop words so amusing and powerful that the lamp is turned on.

Power Steering, you have a sense of humor to which I am learning to adjust. Now, please, may I put my head back on the pillow?

"Your soul mate, somewhere, is still awake, and sending thought messages by his gift of ESP."

Well, in a miracle moment, I'm sending a message, "Today is all spent." My nodding head falls on the pillow, even though the lamp is still on.

Tomorrow I'll get a flashlight, or I will just take my little emergency battery lantern to bed with me. It's awfully bright, brighter than me tonight. Okay, little lantern, Thought Arms are powerful, but they just don't warm my cold feet.

Laughing, me too!

Oh my goodness! Writer's Council just popped out of the sleeping closet, and I have another set of hours in planning. 4:30 a.m.

"Good Night."

INTERVENTION

Is there an intervention taking place for everyone in the ability to sense and feel this inner intuitive? I believe we all have this gift, but the choice of exercising it is like being placed on a balance scale of weights.

The thought so delicate that it has only a microsecond to choose the direction of use. I look at the little kitty treats bag: It's called, "Temptations." It's really easy to dispel the nudge to respond to intuition and just let it disappear.

In my immediate, I had my breakfast ready for the spoon to soothe the open lips of need. However, the urgent beckoning of this little article to be written made the pen stronger than the spoon.

See how easy this little gift of intervention can add great luster to your life? It is like my "Iris" experience of yesterday. I spotted an unusual white iris from my car. Just minutes earlier, an angel had whispered that name in my ear. But in the rushing car was the devilish temptation not to bother. It would require more than seconds. I would have the duty to take it from the photo's digital form all the way to a framed canvas. The angel's intervention spurred me to action. I trusted the intuitive.

Now the framed Iris honors the memory of a young man, a living angel in heaven. He loved irises in his short, artistic life. My decision created a grand celebration of life for an angel who hangs it on his heavenly wall.

Thank you, Lord.

Chapter 5: The Edge of Time

TAKING TIME

We often forget to take time to do something for others even after they have given of themselves in serving kindness. Today, I was blessed with a big hug by a sweet dining hostess, a senorita who has a gift of language and smiles. My taco was perfect, with lots of extra cheese, and, in leaving, I noticed the beautiful Christmas tree sitting all decked against a kitchen walkway.

I asked the senorita, "May I take your picture with the Christmas tree?" She smiled, and I snapped the smartphone picture. For several years, my daughters and I have had lunch here, but I had never seen the hostess' name tag or had asked her name. Today, yes I did, and then she gave me a big hug. You see, individuals need to be recognized. Then she asked, "How old are you?" I laughed and said, without any predetermined response, "In this age, we don't measure age by the chronological clock, but by the age of endurance."

We both laughed and shared another hug. Taking time, yes, it is so valuable.

WREATHS AND LEAVES

Holiday decorations shining brightly in the winter sun. Drawing the eyes upward to green circles of pine and red ribbons. A camera eye could see details that the photographer didn't. Until, in a digital second, cropping into symmetry, there appeared two beautiful oak leaves winging within inches of the fingers of pine. So unexpected in appearance, like life filled with brimming blessings and surprises.

Books fill libraries, but Mother Nature is constantly filling our lives with beauty beyond any bindings. We bind this beauty in digital images in our hearts or in the magical telephones carried in our purses, pockets or hands. Discovery of the oak leaves in flight spell movement caught to be shared. Visual delight in finding autumn leaves, a colorful signature that reminds us that yesterday's beauty still remains. Now the oak leaves clinging to a Christmas wreath become another of earth's treasures.

A lamp pole and street sign left a mark too. On the curb rested a shadow that seemed out of place. I stepped past it to leave it undisturbed. Then intuitive came to rest upon my heart, and the camera allowed this surprise of shadow to emerge. The shadow of the cross, for which Christ was born to wear in the season of Easter, sprung to view, reminding me also of the approaching springtime only a few months away. I understood the meaning of this heaven's shadow that each human being has an infinity beyond this curbside station of here and now.

Later, caught by the lens of my eye and not by camera, appeared in the sky a perfect butterfly-shaped cloud with sun shining behind it to allow its winging into my heart. Butterflies, wreaths, ribbons, leaves and shadow of the cross: earthly treasures revealed through intuitive color filters.

"Oh, my!"

CATALOG

A tiny catalog arrived and received my glance and setting aside. The thought pictures remained for memory storage, however. It highlighted passionately pictorial lore and beckoning for the mountains of Peru and Bolivia. The catalog remained in a stack of wonders.

Until came a surging moment of Christmas, and the nagging thought of finding the little catalog hounded me. The man who established this international project was a college handshake and great speaker, along with his son, now a student, also. Years in the growing, his Heifer Project had become a worldwide network to feed starving people by supplying them animals for a self-sustaining livelihood. So my eyes wandered through the thoughts of sending a gift of a couple of chicks, lambs, goats, or half a heifer. Well, which two quarters of a heifer should that be? Front or back, or just plain look for a different animal of intrigue? So I settled on a llama because of the strong endurance of these animals. But how much? A quarter of a llama, that's kind of a crippling sense. Half felt half-hearted, but then three quarters was getting lukewarm.

The best feeling came just now with the selection of a whole, four-sure-footed llama to be going to a family in Peru or Bolivia. That's a warm fuzzy feeling hard to find, but suddenly arriving.

The page that quoted the cost was shining with these words, "Light Up a Life with Llama!". So, dear reader, out beyond mountains of unimaginable splendor, a baby llama is being born into the household of humanity. Maybe it will bring a degree of warmth that this moment has given me.

It is amazing how catalogs of months' past might spring into the season of Christmas! Thank you, Power Steering, for finding my pen and enabling me to reach a higher mountain than I ever would have climbed!

OVERWHELMED

Strangulation of breath when words just won't stop flowing. Overwhelmed, I am in a mansion without walls at the foot of steps ascending to upper echelons. Could this be the stairway to another world of creativity? I sense universes surrounding space of the unknown. I am overwhelmed by wonder and feelings!

I do know that I am not at the base of a ladder of negativity; rather, I feel the escalating steps moving with optimism to be shared. Can this pen rest, or will it just keep rushing like a flooding river? No answer arrives in my moments of breathless excitement. Please don't pause the use of language when life just wants to go exploring, an inner voice tells me. A jungle of wonder and an overwhelming desire to discover the next unknown! Oh my, destiny at the top of a single staircase! I begin the climb without looking down.

REBOOT

It could mean in storm mode, "Put your boots on again, or have them standing at the ready."

This writing moment is blurred between the misty flurries of winter and the wished-for tropics of my dreams. I want to reboot purpose into my own design. I can draw upon my passions to sort my desires among the gifts that life provides me to find the ones with deepest impact. Power Steering will direct my paths of sharing. Mine is a reboot of energy and enthusiasm that will power me to follow my guided paths.

Discernment removes the barriers to new waves of thinking. Reboot your brain cells to accept great joy and wonder in blades of truth that enable you to construct a little heaven in your earthly spaces. You will find the energy to move in positive directions.

ROOTS OF RETURN

Roots of return draw strongly upon the heart of soul. Remembrance gives birth to strong wonder which creates an inner desire to refresh in a special place of long ago. The call may beckon across the miles and mountain peaks from the youth of beginning.

The distance is great, but the yearning builds and the feelings may become overwhelming.

Time sweeps the clear path for the doing, and the mountains suddenly have closer proximity. The when and how will soon be answered, but there's no question in discerning that the roots of the call are deep within the well of self.

How much to take there? How much to leave behind for the future return on another day? How long to stay, how soon to leave, all answers come within the timing of God's plan!

Soul jarring surprise!

SEEDS

Creative seeds are sown during life experiences, and some are crushed by the plow of conformity. But some find roots in nourishing sunlight and loving care.

Falling golden leaves of autumn, caught on the wind, begin their final dance. So beautiful, this season unmatched in strength and beauty!

The little word-capsules capture memories of this day. Do you hear the rustle of movement as seasons turn within the cycles of a year? In each one, joy embarks again eagerly on a journey to the next bend in our Power Steering road. Take a deep breath of the moment, savor it and share.

In the fall, do you see the countless blessings falling like the leaves? We can catch them in baskets of miracles.

Find a perfect leaf, and stencil it for a stationary glimpse when winter creeps a little closer.

SEEDS OF COURAGE

Planting seeds in whatever hemisphere requires acts of faith and effort. The unseen will sprout to provide nourishment, just like the sowing of encouragement nourishes the soul of humanity.

Powerful seeds of thought raise existence into new realms of happiness. We don't necessarily have to jump into the rapids and feel the turbulent currents of events; rather, we can find little ponds of reflection in our inner depths. Reflecting light brings new and shining moments, un-muddied by the cloudy sediments of past events.

Hello, little soul of energy, truth and happiness!

Take samples of the soil along your journey. Till the soul within to reveal layers not previously measured. Then plant in the proper places the seeds of courage that will grow into super-foods of strength for facing new adventures.

Try sitting motionless, holding a cup of blessings. Let the stirrings within rest. That's life in the germination process for a new birth of enlightenment. Live on the edge of a seed bed to reap the harmony and beauty of a new age.

As for me, today the pen and thought are connected. I just may graduate to another page...maybe even a new book. Softly a period is placed rather than a question mark.

Chapter 6: Journey's Map

WONDER

The wonder of life impulses us to journey to the edge of surprise. Textbooks list the "Seven Wonders of the World," but these edifices are visual. The invisible beauties of life lie in stories of humanity in undesignated places and time. Through these, we encounter awesome experiences and meet great faces along our highways of living.

Are there hands you didn't shake or congratulations you didn't make to people for their accomplishments on the family trees they've climbed? Are there smiles of recognition that you have not bestowed on someone passing by? These may be lost opportunities to visit a wonder of the world.

These moments of wonder, when joy fills the human breast, are blessings of magnitude given by God. There's a rhythm to living that we can develop that tunes us to notice these joyous markers on our highway of life We need only to pause and read the story on each. Then WONDER begins to shape your personal reality.

Thank you, Lord, for my blank page suddenly filled this morning through another power steering venture of faith.

TIME IS RUNNING AWAY

When solid sleep is suddenly interrupted by an awakening pen: The title, "Time Is Running Away," produces an urgency to think about things still undone!

A moment of yesterday returns. I noticed a young woman with earbuds in place. She had been entranced for an hour and a half by her computer. The intuitive spoke, "Give her a note as a little silent departing thought." *Have a wonderful afternoon* sprang onto the card, and I silently slipped away from her library table. She looked up and smiled as this little recognition had moved her suddenly into awareness of a kind expression. We never know if these little acts of thoughtfulness, ever so small or short in doing, give a lift to others who are weighed down by the loads of life. Time speaks ever so softly and flees. Our thoughtful acts must move quickly.

It's true: Time never stops. It rolls onwards as tides rise and fall, storms begin and end, and breaths of life rush to their numbered conclusion. But the fleeting shirttails of moments grasped to share a kindness are remembered always like savory foods.

Today my fascination with this lesson comes on the tip of a ballpoint pen. *The mind is intricate*, I reflect. The surge of urgency relaxes into quiet awareness.

I think of life as a weave of events into shapes I can see and reflect upon. In this mindfulness class, I recall something said yesterday: "Look at the beautiful tapestry having been woven on a loom and shared on the library walls!" Aha moment! I took the camera and asked permission of two ladies working effortlessly. One was weaving on a loom with a shuttle and the other smoothly arranging another strand on a spinning wheel.

They gave permission while their eyes continued to focus on their creative designs. The photos were taken and their beauty shared with a fleeting smile of appreciation. Gratitude spoken and evidence made in our digital world when time continues to spin away.

Oh, the glories of a nighttime memory caught by both camera and pen! If the moment isn't caught and treasured, it will disappear. Now let's run with time and watch to see who becomes witnesses for JOY!

BAGGAGE

An old song: "Pack up your troubles in an old kit bag and smile!"

Emerging baggage at the airline terminal, train station or bus depot is usually with your own card tag or masking tape identification. Well, then there's no need to worry, because the bags belong to you. However, what about the baggage others dump on your desk or shoulders? Shrug off this junk mail, remove your name and address, and plunk it all into a big garbage bag! I just placed one in the bathtub temporarily, but even if water were in the tub, I know that the bag will not float.

Empty these at the trash removal spot, feel the relief of lighter loads. That's the way we should feel after disposing negative thoughts. This isn't psychology; it's just keeping life simple.

"Raindrops keep falling on my head", another lyric so memorable! It's refreshing to feel the delete button clicked! In my baggage, I'd sure like to pack a new outfit and leave something else at Good Will.

HARNESS

In old-fashioned days of transportation, the carriage-and-horse times, harnesses were visible means of control. Today's generations have no memory of the leather strappings and the blinders for the eyes.

But invisible harnesses today restrict the conscious efforts of chosen professions. The time schedule is in charge of arranging the pleasures of eating, sleeping and even the gentle strokes of caring. Ouch! You probably have never thought of that kind of harness. Neither have I, until now. But my unharnessed pen is alive and well and enjoying its flow out of retirement and into action. Smiling is unharnessing the inner treasures of life!

Don't think of harness like a conveyor belt on which move goods stamped uniformly to the consumer. Instead, make tables of contents or indices to shape your organization. In this way you have guides, not restrictions. These can be modified as pages are edited. Just enable your creative tree branches to ascend to more stratospheric heights. From the higher limbs you can take deep breaths of life and have clearer views!

TUMBLEWEED

Whirlwinds of tumbleweed thought might be turned on and off as if by a light switch.

And the hunger and thirsting of morning might be satisfied by simply adding sunlight of happy experiences. As this morning gilds early, a song of Sunday energy developed to pick up the garden hose. To hit the jet stream or shower toggle depended upon the herbal or floral structure. The freshness of dew and spray mixing helped to nourish fragile life, and I relaxed again.

No longer tumbleweed, because the Power Steering of today began at the water faucet and nozzle. Effort without hurry or instructions.

ROOTS

Roots run deep, and tonight it seems as though they run all the way back to Scotland (and Ireland, too). The Scotts from Scotland and the Crosses from Ireland are the ancestors of my birth. They melded in their new country, and the abundance of land became their legacy. No time traveler could ever find all their descendants, unless Power Steering found all roads leading home.

It's a growing season now, when our culture has omitted the artisans who formed the fabric that make up each of us. But, thanks to them, we are solid, staunch and determined to take heart in where we come from.

Power Steering you have some real heavy tires, and the terrain may be rugged, but so are we! Our forefathers never felt apathy or complacency, as they had much to do to build our great country. A professional of high respect gave this author a parting statement: "Know thyself."

Do we really meet this commission?

COUNTRY TIME

Country time and sunshine, after seventeen days of sultry, rain-swept skies. Recognizing the summer aura fading and wishing to capture the last orange roses, pink cornflowers and fading arrays of green.

This is a hamlet jazzing with a hardworking community where licking fingers expresses gratitude for the meal that has been served. There is joy that everyone should indulge that comes from magnificent lives of rich stories within knowing hearts.

A smiling waitress brings a piece of homemade coconut cream pie and fresh coffee. She wishes to share this little piece of America with a fork full of whipped cream.

A secret of sitting in a window seat that looks out from old-fashioned wall decors, a spinning ceiling fan, and a chalkboard filled with rainbow colored chalk-goodies. A comfort of things to make company with this scene is a good book and (as always) a pad of writing paper to capture this heavenly moment. Even the huge food service truck parked outside and marked "PERFORMANCE" is equal to the task of "Best!"

THE INSTAGRAM

Guardian angels sitting on the shoulder and whispering to the pen. Speaking a thought language for all to seek. Words flowing from the wireless waves of the inner brain to compute. There's a wave of God's genius that oscillates like a warm hand shake. It's not an electrical charge surging; it is more like a recharging of a battery at the ready.

Questions arise to wonder: What? When? Where? Why? Then again "Why me?" Can you answer these questions? Do you shake or shrug your shoulders as inquiry about the next endeavor to pursue?

In town, out of town or all around the town, there are always messages of need. To feed the hungry by word or deed. Or is it understanding to just be a listener to how far each has come along his or her individual journey? Do they need shoes to carry them further, or just a smile to feed and nourish the soul?

Wherever today's adventures take you, look into the eyes of everyone you meet and smile. Give a silent greeting that says, "You are special!"

FRAGRANCES

There's sensory mystery in the fragrances that evoke memories. I remember a long gone friend who would give me a hug and say, "You make me feel like a teenager again." That wasn't any romantic encounter; rather, it was the fragrance of the "Wind Song" perfume that he remembered at his teen years' high school prom. All that could be said was, "Thank you for such a lovely compliment from memory's time." But when cancer took the reins of this gifted medical professional, I cried.

Today, there's a fragrance of cherry blossoms and springtime melted into a wax dish. As it sits on the dresser, it is a creation asking to be recognized as a gift from the artisan's hands. It won't melt on its stand, but its fragrance evokes memories of the little moments of life that have lain dormant until magic came to visit. Its scent lingers on my fingers, and, although I leave not a fingerprint or trace of DNA, it leaves me with a breath of another season wishing to be discovered.

This is my genuine appreciation sent to my sister who shared the chair with me when we listened to "Let's Pretend." She knows how to soften life's little birthdays.

IT'S OKAY

It's okay that in reading a book filled with Old Scottish roadways and descriptive scenery that these can drift into the fog. The author felt so compelling that a friendship seemed to come from kin folk. Her woven mystery of the Highlands and Lowlands was a tapestry from her magical memory, as she now lives in the Far East. A question unanswered or even noted is the epilogue. It's okay to be caught in the lines and between the lines of shared impressions. However, there's a loss when the last page is reached. So here's to A.D. Scott, a fantastic author of Scottish heritage, whose novel, *The Low Road,* caught me up in hope and loss and, perhaps, reality.

LIVING FULLY

Patterns in living begin to form a profile of effort and accomplishments. It's a collection of work adventures that are explored, achieved and then put in the past. Some are chosen by need, and some you were chosen to do. Combinations of many interests may be explored in the work cultures over a lifetime. In the educational pathway, each experience is a building block to a new choice.

My own personal reaching led to many opportunities. I began my work adventure first dishing ice cream and measuring out too much of the profits for the eager customers. On to be a legal secretary and getting into court house proceedings, and then to work for a State Forestry department, where hiking on field trips led to learning the many types of trees. But I turned down a job with the State Department of Forestry. All these were short excursions before I began the college climb on the steps to higher learning. The initial excursions of work were interruptions by some measure, but to me working brought such a joy.

College times were filled with study and being secretary for a great theologian. Two years of exercising writing of this man's great sermons. I took courses in philosophy, where I endured getting a grade of B because the Professor expected more growing to happen.

Long story of educational intervals and getting a GS-3 for government work. A challenge of a lot more learning, and transfers interrupted that. Oh my, reading and running blue prints for the National Fire Guard Co. in the suburbs of Chicago. All were little stepping stones that whetted my appetite to learn more.

Looking back on the Chicago experience, the hardest moment was a Good Friday when the store closed and no one had even thought to say, "Lunch will be a long one." Getting caught in this cold winter encounter was a mid-west learning that calendars and the time clock were to be on the radar.

Ah, the richness of living! I recall driving with great running gusto to plow through heavy snow in Mother's new car. Up a great hill I went and continued to climb, flying past the pasture that was always a frightening springtime experience of the great bull at the fence. Too close for comfort! On in the memories, to the year that the road was blocked with cornstalks on Trick or Treat Night. These little rich recollections keep rolling along on the back roads of my memory.

Come to think of it, I showed courage and quick thinking when a new position to go to a Chicago Publishing Company was offered. Turning down this position for love, I began to recognize that the need for the personal and professional must be in balance.

I am wondering now what my Scottish grandparents would have thought of their red-haired, green-eyed granddaughter. I can remember my sandy-haired Grandpa with powerful hands and a wonderful laugh exchanging marvelous stories with his yodeling neighbor.

This is only a little piece of my life resume, but in here lie clues to the experiences that helped me build strength and determination. Catch another glimpse on another page of recollection. Running up the stair case of experiences, have you thought to record your own experiences? Perhaps being alone for a little while will bring out your welling memories. Thank you, Power Steering, for this quiet time of thought.

FIRST IMPRESSION

"Smash words" sounds like words made into mush.

Mush is cornmeal and water boiled and stirred until thickened as an old country recipe. Thick mush can be served hot as porridge like in "The Three Bears" story or broken into pieces and fried. Some like it served with syrup or apple butter. Someone just might have swallowed the word "fair" to make room for the smashing taste of "good!"

Okay, with the fast rolling internet and the www portion, I'll check out the real Smashwords menu and look for the great success that writing can now bring. No intention to smash the words here! I am just having fun redistributing the word meaning, and now I have a wakeup call for success. Words can be hot, cold, boiled and fried. A rage or rave, it has been a fun play on words and a little game to entertain me.

PARKWAY OF SPRING

The Colonial Parkway was dressed in the best April apple green and lime green! The wind softly embraced the lacy dogwood overhanging the view. I was hunting to take the perfect picture on this long-ago revolution highway.

The mission for today was to find wisteria in luxuriant lavender beauty amid its tangled roots of time.

Turning in to a little roadway, a surprise met this photographer's gaze. Why was there a lawn chair sitting beside the road and a bottle of water?

Shortly, a little lady emerged with a Canon cannon camera propping a giant lens. In stopping with curiosity, I asked, "What are you looking at?" She pointed to a distant forest of pine and a huge square nest. Appreciating my interest, she said, "That's an eagles' nest that I've looked at for five years. There are two babies up there now, and I saw Momma a while ago."

"Did you get pictures?"

"Oh yes!"

"Are you a professional photographer?"

"Oh no, I just take 100 digital pictures and save maybe one!"

Introductions were exchanged. We were a half hour on the edge of the Yorktown Battlefields with its redoubts in the distance. We took pictures, shared the best viewing spots, and I found the fresh wisterias here too. Cotton clouds darting here and there changed the sunlight.

The little hostess had been there five hours and decided it was time to go.

For my collection of precious moments to ponder, there is one of the mother Bald Eagle returning and sitting on a sharp angle to keep an eye on her babies. She was maybe fifteen feet above their big home.

Pictures from the 35mm Minolta captured this in a distant view, and, hopefully, magnification will bring these birds of freedom to a picture frame.

In retrospect, it is to say, "Intuitive and Power Steering are in flight again!"

POTENTIAL

Power Steering is a teacher in the process of acknowledgement. It holds the key to just letting go of the forces known as hurry, scurry and demand! It can be as quiet as a kitty purring beside a braided rug. The moment can be savored, allowing thoughts to become woven from a quiet spool.

This is a Wednesday morning beginning. I sit quietly to explore the potential of the day. There's no restlessness. The day holds potential to discover. Not even a raging hurricane in the far distant waters will disturb this moment now! This is the embrace of the NOW. Have you developed this skill in your reservoir of talents? Unlock this mechanism of quiet reflection. There's no syllabus of direction. This is opening wide the universe to find for yourself!

Author's sharing to assist you in discovering your own power steering movements.

Beneath the surface of living, you have been constructing a steady foundation upon which to build strength.

"Thank you, Lord."

PERFECT TIMING

Power Steering certainly has perfect timing, worth every bit of time to mention. My longtime favorite little country garage always takes care of checking the car pulse, timing, and air for tires to breathe. So this morning I called and heard, "Sure, come on in at 1:00 p.m.!"

Oh, perfect, it's Friday, and another item can be checked off the list. In walking into their office, I saw their vacation sign, "LEAVING TOMORROW!" The pretty blonde young lady (and a former student) greeted me with, "Perfect timing!" She's even wearing a "Power - Pride" T-shirt. Wow! The heavens do exist above this rotating planet.

"Thank you, Lord."

NIGHT TIME STI|RRINGS

Reading the past brings a sense of having reached a plateau after a long climb. There's a time to refresh the spirit of accomplishment regardless of the altitude. Speechless with feelings of numbness! It's not the weather outside or the inside temperature affecting me; rather, it is the whole wonder of the distance of what lies ahead. A hiker would have a map and compass for direction, but power steering in charge can leave a dizzy feeling of not being at the controls. Is this a flight into the future or a fantasy of a writer's trial-and-error?

Time out for rest, and check the best headings for tomorrow! Perhaps just the strength of the purple pen and Higher Power will divulge the mysterious steps of the next climb. I hear a door close. Perhaps this is my elevator going up?

GREEN LIGHT PACT

Before beginning this green light roll, washing the hands of the past is important. It is time to make a pact. What is a pact? Is it like packing a suitcase for a grand trip, or is it a heavier deal to keep a promise?

A pact with the Lord should be in capital letters!

Teetering long ago after surgery and a 58% chance, I made a pact with the Lord. Here it comes!

"Dear Lord of great healing power, grant healing to me in this moment in time, and I'll share my writing with your ailing world!" The healing took place, and slowly the energy to share has built. We aren't always quick to do what has been promised, but courage becomes our green light to go forward even though the roadway ahead has no signs of direction. The highway of life for all of us is a mystery in the fog of time.

Legacy is written and packed. Others carry this suitcase left behind. For me, I have the sunshine of surprise that this endeavor is written on the line today!

Alarm clock sounded!

"Thank you, Lord!"

Chapter 7: Intuitive Reaching to Infinity

SIMPLE WRITING REMNANTS

Writing may have sprung from a deep inner yearning into the Stone Age hieroglyphics carved in heavy strokes on stone. Or maybe into the papyrus and parchment still hidden in old earthenware jugs. The today of yesteryear is seen in the old-fashioned manuscript in cursive writing which today's youth have had little time to learn. Instead, the evolving of life has developed the texting and email journeys of wireless time.

The deep inner yearning to speak when there's no one to read or to listen is still pulsed in the quiet of the Master's touch, when through power steering, the hand expresses the mind of body. Thoughts contained by a fragile veil of an inner world break through, and a written line gets recorded. There's no conscious manufacture of this instant; rather, yearning powers the delivery of this fragile gift to share.

Think of the Stone Age hearts in search for words, when pictures became the form of long-lived expression. Journey back and suddenly appreciate this miracle of expression. Could it be like the Zen tangle of art, a manifestation, too, of inner thoughts? Life holds mazes of thoughts, and from within comes the urgency of freedom to breathe, live and write.

Architects of human history who strive for immortality build mansions of thought. Living words pronounced in the Master's love transcend the walls of torn history. We become master weavers in the power of God's own time.

JUST SITTING

"Just sitting" sounds like a nothing item in the schedules of hurry. In this morning of stillness, the motionless momentum of body and soul have reached this position. The urgency of the mind has slowed thanks to the resting of night and finds a new edge of peace.

Branches of thought meander around the stacks of waiting and find amusement in the 85% discounts of unopened magazines.

Moment of discernment shows new ways to organize work. I leave it so as not to stir up worry.

Just sitting, be it on the stair-step of planning or on the deck of ready-to-roll again, is a gift of mini-vacation from often found pressures building. Just sitting can bring new construction to purpose and shed new lighting on life's treasure houses. It's like the white flaking of paint on the picket fences of colonial times. The fences remain that way, and life goes on. These are gateways unexplored, and beyond the boxwood hedge, we've found a new beginning.

Just sitting, and a little smile rises. Only a few minutes have been taken for this luxury of "time out!"

Try it!

THE INTUITIVE GYMNASTICS

This title has up and down thoughts like a trampoline in use. The occurrence of the intuitive can never be anticipated, but the response to it is a choice. It's not an artifact, but a fact requiring a delicate balance of doing the right thing at the right time.

Here's an illustration of the intuitive in conflict with the battle of "no". A need was sensed to send a g-mail to a precious member who is as close as an Indian blood brother. It felt like, "Yes" send," against "No, don't send. You are being a bombarding bother."

"Oh, okay..."

And again this morning: *Should I send a note? Oh, well, maybe just a little subject, "Sunshine!" A smiley face won't hurt. Or, should there be the business of continuing the check off list of publishing requirements?* Finally, giving in to the list idea, off went the new Table of Contents.

The day spun smoothly into the speed limit to get a shampoo and set and maybe a cut, too. *Yes, definitely a cut too!* So as the intuitive went gently off to a silent corner of the right hemisphere thinking, it was like taking a breather from the heavier exercise of worry.

A little later, the "nudge" hit, and in checking the g-mail, there was the response like a ray of light through the venetian blinds. Yes, the happy gremlins I had sent drew a response of, "I have been working so hard and have been depressed about a family member's diagnosis." Words raced out again this time with encouragement and love for this family of precious souls.

Perhaps now you can fathom how little things like sending a thought of love and encouragement can get someone else past the drapes of worry and despair. Intuitive Gymnastics, there's a partnership in continuing our *Power Steering 2*. Thank you, Lord, for great healing and compassion. Of this we are all responsible to perform our part.

REACHING

"What and where shall we go or do today, Lord"? Is that expressed sufficiently to be understood by the pulsing heart, the unhurried feet and the pursuit of wisdom? The unstoppable moments for savoring, saving and sharing. Today is brand new, and we've never lived this one before!

What will happen to bring indelible thoughts into light?

Is there an itching shoulder of past healing reminding us that the angel on the shoulder just might be dancing with delight?

Even the signal to rest may be the recipe for waiting! What? Where? Why? Perhaps these three questions are presented just to be acknowledged as always, ready to be lived, expressed or to be filled with surprise. Life is wonderful! Get up, get going, and get ready for answers so personal that are between you and God to share.

On this December Sunday morning of the Grand Illumination in our colonial town, I visualized a frail little lady in church and saw her face quiet and still. *I must go to church and see her*. Yes, she was seated in her favorite spot with her husband nearby. I told her in greeting, "I could see your face, and you are the reason I came this morning." She looked and tilted her head in reply. "I'm so glad to see you. I had eye surgery this week, and I have only one eye to see now!" I held her hand and said, "But you have one beautiful eye, and your wonderful face and smile are a blessing to all of us.

"Oh, I'm so glad you said that."

These were Judy & Bill, our church pillars, holding strong in faith and love.

Later, a lady whom I have meant to call for several months and say, "Let's go to lunch soon." She didn't answer her phone, but the voice machine reported, "I'm in the hospital."

Searching for where she might be found was a challenge, but finally a phone number registered as a possible location. Searching the computer and making phone calls, finally I reached her area: "Skilled Living!" said the responder. She transferred the call. Her phone rang, but no answer.

But then a nurse answered. My friend had had a stroke. I had taken her to lunch in September just before she left to take the train to Charleston to visit old friends. There it happened, a stroke that brought a major change to her active life. We chatted, and the slur in her voice could be detected, but cheerful conversation brought more fluency. Yes, Lord, the intuitive has been rewarded with a renewing friendship and encouragement to one who needs it.

There are needs that we often ignore, and these might have been two on the same day. Guidance is such a fragile thing to offer, but it is so needed. Yes, what and where have been answered. Truly it has been Grand Illumination Day, celebrating eighteenth century holidays and also the heart of sharing.

WAVE LENGTHS

The sense of intuitive can be a driving power to reach even long distances.

Thoughts travel power lines that require no permission to erect across rivers. No sound, only the warmth of discovering wave lengths untarnished by weathering elements. A pattern without shape, but bound by caring.

Wave lengths that need no measuring can zoom through tunnels in mountains and surface in sunrises or sunsets. Eyes to behold the beauty of knowing. This untouchable feeling travels from intangible into the tangible. Nothing can stop wave lengths of energy and enthusiasm! These are braided into the living and breathing of every individual. Catch the wave length of happiness, and you are the picture of smiling joy!

LOST IN THE MOMENT

The title has just been born from the joy of catching a breath of springtime in December grandeur!

When a new season arrives before its normal appearance, I find cherry blossoms in lacy beauty! Lost in the moment, walking blocks to get the perfect view of sky through floral branches interlaced in colorful splendor. Lost in the moment, when the camera and I reach beyond the street sounds and forgotten passersby, who may be wishing that they were free to grasp the moment, too. The branches of cherry blossoms, so delicate in color and shape!

Yes, lost in the moment, but forever capturing it in the digital eye and in mine. The essence of peace with little brushes of wind dancing. Lost, yes, and found again, a moment of rapture that pleasures the inner soul. Daring to cross busy streets and many lives just to find a touch of heaven. Lost in the moment, a treasure dressed in the many shades of creativity!

Thank you Lord for this gift of sight.

THE INVISIBLE UMBRELLA

The invisible umbrella keeps raising and lowering like the raindrops of protection. It's that infinite moment when creativity is revealed, and everyone under the canopy feels the freedom to share. It's like a Writers Haven. There's no criticism in sharing, and the moments of little life exposures become accepted as examples of creative genius. Defenses are non-existent. Someone says, "There's no internet, iPhones, texting or television", and, so, the moments have been filled with laughter. Soft music has added a magical background to this expression.

It is like old-time visits with friends when common wave lengths are measured in units that are alive and personal and wireless inventions are silent. This invisible umbrella is available for discovering like-minded people, who just might become your lifetime friends. Moments are shared and protected as God's Blessing is revealed.

HEART OF TIME

Within the pulse-beat of time unmeasured by human eye, there is an all knowing that comes from Higher Power.

We needn't worry about this within our human breast, as Higher Power holds the length of destiny. To wonder is good, as awareness brings focus to purpose. We rise above the everyday calendar page into the satisfaction of reaching toward best.

Focus shows in our eyes. We see clearly reflected the penetrating gaze of others who are interested. Guides for the day are special. They may be found opening a door for strangers, or they may be discovered again in familiar faces from past experiences. The quality of exchanges may be immeasurable in delight. Right place and right time is a touch of destiny.

The impulse to judge is not on the calendar. It's the unexpected that again thrives within hearts.

Thank you Lord, for preserving breath and heart to give energy.

HARMONY

Soundscapes abut the walls of music and deliver measures of easy listening. Wordscapes, too, can please the minds' eye and make home in our hearts of peace.

An endeavor that this writer seeks to capture through the essence of joy-filled moments that retrace the reader's own journey:

Climbing imaginary mountains to great plateaus of inner vision, leading to growth. Streaming thoughts bound on threads of wonder, suggesting new, uncharted goals. It is so important to be in touch with your own sensory brilliance!

All these images begin to erase the tension of circular cells within your brain. Your vision clears to see treasures of your own discovery. You find pathways through this beautiful world of sight and sound. You hear little echoes of encased memories, suddenly emerging on musical tones that vibrate health and happiness.

You, the reader, may wonder why am I holding this thought so close, and it just may mean that we all share the stage on the platform of life. Together, we make harmony that reaches out to be acknowledged, like the works of artists and great masters of our cultures.

Little moments captured in the mist of feathery fern. We are the culture that each of us live, share and love.

IN TOUCH WITH SELF

The title may seem very selfish in first impression, but, in a second thought, do we ever give this an open door to explore?

What does intuitive say to this self within the boundaries of height, weight and address? Simple, silly little nothings get ignored, because self runs a race everyday with the should-have-done or the should-do lists.

When the kitty comes to say goodnight, he receives a happy toenail scratch and then gets a temptation-seafood-medley treat. It's the listening to the little crunch and soft whiskers meeting the hand that make keeping in touch special. Each of us are special and unique in the great cosmos of planets' spinning turns. The Creator of All has given each of us tools of sensitivity to discover the little things, and He blesses us, too, with the big things.

Perhaps this would have never been written if my link to the outside world didn't just stop this afternoon. The computer is still able to light up and receive incoming emails, but the sending out is on the refusal mode. Tomorrow may bring answers, but for tonight only the green package of kitty treat temptations helps to recognize that it's never too late to discover self. You'll find it a glorious treat to meet yourself. How about that for a little goodnight wish? All systems are off, and eyelids also await their closing down.

P.S. The computer remedy was a new battery required in the wireless keyboard. We, too, need to battery-up for energizing!

Chapter 8: The Shining Soul

SOUL REACHING

Deep in the soul of search lies an indwelling command to listen for little urgings of worth. The spirituality that is hidden within the human form longs for its discovery. There is no need of a robe for warmth, as the awakening is already within the protective spirit of inner life.

The wordless verbalism that is growing stronger rises to the surface of Now. It's not a coughing up of hurt; rather, it is a warm balm of anointing prayer. Soul-search becomes soul-sharing, and it holds no roadmap.

The inner companionship has the precious name of "Savior". Guiding angels deliver unseen touches to the elbow in encouragement to continue on. "On to where?" is a pathway spelling mystery.

So strange, in the morning of dark before daylight, even the sound of the pen awakens the snoozing Persian cat who has never before come to lay beside these sheets. Pausing to see the resting spirit, I recognize its outstretched feline outline so near and warm to mine.

A MENTAL WALK TODAY

Beyond the doorstep lies the great signature of Mother Nature. She hasn't started yet to smile and begin to melt her Winter touch. The time of yesterday brought great blasts of wind, rain, snow and ice.

Tree limbs are dressed in heavy snow, and form-bending arms reach toward earth's bosom. Leaves wear lacy ice strands as if woven in beauty from a winter loom. Mother Nature has said, "Peace on Earth, my children!" By her measure, even the flooding tides met stoppage at some doorsteps.

It is time to recognize that blessings can melt right into your being. Awareness of Grace is like finding a friend. It melts away the hard knocks of negativity, depression and loneliness! The time is at hand to allow the warmth of God's love to blanket your life with faith and hope.

The steadiness of deep breaths releases the hold of stress. The grip of season has brought you to your walk with Mother Nature.

BLESSINGS

Digging deeper into the miracle of blessings: So many may have passed by unrecognized. As you journeyed through life, did you notice these small-to-huge blessings that made your life richer by experiences? Or, were these missed because of fragility, like tiny woven spider webs? Perhaps they might have been seen if the fog or dew had preserved them seconds longer.

These blessings are real, once understood as miracles of vision. It is like my awakening from a deep sleep of surgery with new eyes of implants, carefully prescribed and gently placed. Even the nurse who cared for me pre-and-post surgery was suddenly at the right place and time! She was a parent of a precious gifted child whom I had taught. Oh yes, waking and seeing such a miracle of a doctor's gift!

The healing time so short, but in the great surprise, something happened. In the night of just a little time, awakening to white light and the nothingness of sight. One eye blind to the new day! Rushing minutes along the road to the Capitol of our Commonwealth for another surgery. The mystery now of sight returned and focus of clarity to see again and love again the camera of eyes and the lens of digital joy. Yes, thank you, Lord, for the miracle workers who have protected this sensor of sight.

Then my hearing: The gift of hearing so delicate that sound had an unusual intensity and required the finest tuning. Several times, three to be exact, when mastoids were then not fiction. However, the skillful hands of many white-garbed doctors and nurses worked upon me, and from the high ceiling lights I watched the performance of their touch of miracles for my tiny child witness. Memory of what is now called out-of-body experience, and the meaning of the Master's grace enlightened my heart. Recorded now for truth to be shared at the first light of day!

Oh, so many miracles experienced! The touch of higher power felt on an open road in Arizona. The speed was 80, and the towing of a 32-foot Airstream was a smooth run through the night; that is, until three giant "semis" were running tandem and left no space between.

The powerful vacuum created by these night giants caused the jack-knife to begin. With family so dear and time on the short side of a mountain cliff, I said, "Lord, I commend our souls to you!" But the Higher Power of strength began to slow our forward motion, and only the car and water tank made a connection like a handshake. Truly, that night of blessings is forever remembered! The jack-knife of speed, the miracle from above, and then the continuance of driving on through the desert night. I was told that continuing on is supposed to be the remedy to overcome fear. But I remember a questionable adrenalin surge and later exhaustion.

Miracles, yes, so many more, but for tonight, I'll leave those in a precious memory cell to share again another time. Reliving this episode puts the clock in the lime light and draws the drape on another performance on our stage of life.

Thank you for being my audience, and, please, no applause. Just stop to recognize your own blessings of life and love.

TIME

Love comes back multiplied in warmth when it has radiated out to others. The kindnesses sent without expected return are gifts of life in bountiful measure.

Waiting for words to flow toward a river of meaning. Heartfelt moments freely bestowed are heaven's gifts to earthlings. Beating hearts create the rhythm of life's great miracles. Pulsing, radiating joy is seen on the faces of those who experience love. This comes naturally, without posing, in secure moments of sharing. The sharing is our choice.

Look for these moments and discover threads of passion. The extension ladder from heaven to earth balances on a plain of living. Truth becomes beautiful in the soft light of deeds performed without expectation of reward. All can happen in the beauty of time.

3:00 A.M.

Wee hours and early morning chill beckon to reach for the comforter of Wisdom. Stop the questing and curl up for resting. Mind-search has reached slowly-paced minutes, and life's extension has coursed through the body for energizing again. The piercing thought doesn't leave body tattoos; rather, it leaves a trail of sparkles as it ascends to new plateaus. Again, a little sprinkle of Stardust to become the nourishment for sleep.

REACHING INTO SPACE

Orbiting space cameras capture and transmit spectacular views of Milky Way magic. Eye of the camera is much beyond our earthly view of it. The feeling of awe and the recognition that beyond earth's mantle lies so much yet to discover and fathom. The Milky Way leaves us breathless to see its stream of spiraling stars in a beauty unmarked by human footstep. This speaks to the inner soul of conscious thought. The totality of visual peace, un-eroded and picture perfect.

The eyes beyond awaken to witness the space stars twinkling a welcome.

"Hello world! Hello out there, stars in space!"

Truly, the gifts of creativity by our Maker God provide light for love to blossom throughout all seasons for the seekers on planet Earth.

The unseen remains a mystery of hope, faith and enduring love. Thank you, Lord, for revealing your touch of eternity. The sprinkling of star dust reached our planet from the eons of time.

There's Power Steering for all of us to discover.

BONDING

Obeying Power Steering in the realm of supernatural flashes you to a mysterious moment. It arrives in an instant like a space capsule launched in that 3,2,1, lift off. The brilliance of igniting fuel is a blinding beyond comprehension. In the moment of obedience, you feel a bonding unexplained. Could it be a psychic moment when external world and spiritual are united?

It feels like an anointing of warm oil that holds true peace.

The All Powerful has given a little hint of heaven while earth is still spinning.

Seemingly, a mission of discovery is unveiled to you to recall a place where perfect love is. Afterwards, permission to return to terra-firma is granted.

Dear Lord of Creation, inspiration has been ignited again, and your humble servant is trying to comprehend the magnitude of it all. Words require focus. What is the next step? Maybe, this is only the revelation to me of what is, but it's up to someone else to reach for the stars.

"Hello, world! Hello out there, stars in space!"

QUESTION?

Is there a gene of grace hidden within each birth? Perhaps it found nourishment through the umbilical cord to develop into the miracle of a gift from heaven.

God is the great Patriarch of the Universe. By whatever name each religion may bestow, He is the Great Name of the Known. He bestows upon us a heritage that is elusive until the prayer of wonder breaks the shell where our bequeathed knowledge is found.

There is mystery without a totality of answers, but the heart of faith brings revelation to our new awareness.

The edge of day to appears for each to find the Heart of Love embracing us all.

This pen producing the quest for answers to questions and finding the liberating truth without prior design. Freedom to think, ponder and grow in the bursting beauty of time. It's yours, too! Perhaps rest extends to infinity, and soul races to meet destiny's call.

DIMINISHING MEMORY

What an exercise of wakefulness, in closing a manuscript, and a title of this magnitude surfaces!

Our culture is experiencing this epic problem of diminishing memory, and it seems to have no clinical answers.

To venture into this realm just might be called a miracle instead of a Pandora curse. The growing population evidences the phenomenon more and more. But perhaps there may be a blessing to leave negativism out of memory cells while the family and doctors wonder what has taken place.

The blessing may be in finding a new tranquility. Not to be judged by their edging forgetfulness. The key to be found is the why. Let's allow these souls to reach closer to heaven's portal and recognize joy in their positive smiles and their gentler ways of efforts. Let's allow their forgetting hard labors of worry and the confident shoes of success, and let them enjoy the time of today measured in diminishing memory!

Reach out with a new appreciation of these silver streaming souls from the highways and byways of the fast track to allow them space for a comfortable plateau view.

Perhaps the mental cells of worth are slowing, but so is the momentum of their stress. Could this be a miracle of health that is not yet recognized, but is, instead, criticized because we fear the loss of past encounters is not okay?

Soul may be speaking for these beautiful individuals in Memory Clinics, and it is trying to say, "It is okay!"

Dare to resist judging others, and, instead, offer these precious souls new tools to use. Encourage them to paint new creations from the abstract that we might not be able to grasp. Diminishing memory may be cleaning out the mental storehouse of stuff no longer needed.

Celebrate memory of the beautiful and allow this to garner recognition!

With our daring help, our experienced citizens can be bolder instead of older by chronology. Accept this new generation of creative hearts. Love them. Care for them. Let them omit the duties of heavy burdens that memory just really doesn't need.

Labels are no longer required. In their place, we find acceptance of souls' entrance into Joy.

"Whew! A cup of instant coffee will be fine!"

INSPIRATION

Inspiration is rooted in seeds that grow in vines and reach beyond the surface sounds of the roadways. It is invisible, but when one feels it, it is like a microwave being turned on, and the timer is caught in decision: How long must the wave lengths of the mind perform to bring forth the final product of understanding?

Each discovered word is thrust towards creative action. Inspiration is a beautiful element in the design of knowledge. It may appear artificial to some. For others, it's the firm foundation of their lives. The discernment is that little miracles of inspiration exist. Often they go unnoticed.

Stand before a mirror, and, beyond the image, there's the real you with direction for hand to greet and feet to place on the action chart.

Inspiration is the instrument of creativity that surrounds us. It can manifest in the smile to a stranger that says without voice, "Good morning!"

Focus-Discover-Perform.

Inspiration is the invisible being made visible. Little sticky notes can be retrieved in a second to make reminders for further investigation. Inspiration is a tool for the detective who wants a key to a greater dimension called "Happiness."

Power for change comes in the inspiration-magnet attaching to you. A door closes, but thought races ahead, beginning steps in the growth of sensitivity.

Eyelids want to close, but thoughts win!

(Place the cap on the pen, and race for "Save As Is!").

WAITING IN THE SUN

There in the parking lot, waiting beside the car door, a blue precise pen. In picking it up, I found it warm and ready to be recognized for its skills again.

In search of another parking space, no need to hunt, there, too, it was waiting for me. A long walk to the DeWitt Wallace Gallery. The yellow buttercups were like beautiful punctuation marks saying, "Hello!"

Writing is the joy of painting words on a page that float into awareness for others to discover. Waiting is okay. In the waiting time can be warm incubation of thoughts to be shared at the right time and place. Thank you for understanding.

MINI-SURPRISE

Is my life like a bottle filled with mini-pieces of chocolate chunks? My nodding, sleepy question of last night has received an answer this morning.

"Thank you, God," for such a sweet and precious answer after twenty-five years of silence and many evolving events.

The world of fast computers found a familiar face and g-mail address, long searched. There smiling out at me was my twenty-five-year lost friend, originally from New Zealand.

Today, my data phone brought her g-mail and another linking life story. Tears welled with happiness and sadness all mixed, warm and salty like the oceans between us.

Thank you, Lord, for friends across the years. Sharing healing prayers of health for her dear husband. Families having joy and sadness, linked again in memory. To Beverly & Ken with Love.

SILENCE

Where there is silence to the wakened senses, there is space for receiving God's plan. The inner voice can be felt in the thought waves of heaven. Let no anticipation block the coming inspiration. The blinded eyes begin to open to the new creation of peace on earth. Optimism permeates the brain waves to inspire action. It empowers us to become the purpose given for being here and now in this timeline of culture. The gift of free will and choice has awakened strengthening, and Power Steering slips out of park, past neutral and into drive. If the climb is difficult, then the second gear can take its place to meet the challenge. Thought drives the action to make progress possible. The unseen Faith draws new strength from the silence of Mind & Heart united. A oneness of the soul from silence has reached the light of day.

Autumn has been granted entrance into the cycle of seasons. Thank you, Lord, for your timing now!

SPELL BOUND

The LORD is powerful in mysterious ways beyond comprehension of words.

Humbleness lies deep in the artesian well of spirituality, and it bubbles up happiness that cannot be described. This special happiness has the quality to remain with us on the conveyor belt of life, a ribbon of the unseen that, seemingly, has no end.

Tangible when the hard copy is released, and the time capsule is sent heavenward. Quivering shock waves that seem to resonate to unknown hemispheres of exploration. A journey that has reached the horizon of time from the now, radiating into the hearts of humankind.

Power Steering! A divine link to the unknown!

BRAND

Waiting for the next mission of words to ply upon the page. Power Steering has moments of sheer quiet. It ends in praise.

Deep breaths moving from visible into the invisible of time.

There's a sash looped into a collar, and its name is Infinity. Someone coined a powerful label, but, perhaps, they recognized that spirit does flow into infinity.

Today, a good feeling of having obeyed the expression of the continuity of life by our maker, God.

Chapter 9: Midnight Splendor

AT THE WELL

The midnight hour is lost in wonder and delight! It springs forth from the stillness of the mind, heart and soul. The gaining of truth is memory of a well from which the old-fashioned hand pump drew up liquid from hand-shoveled depths in the lime. The effort produced a divine refreshment that years ago people would come from miles around to receive. An old tin was left on a post that the family never touched, but it was the traveler's invitation. Does it still exist where an old Australian pine kept vigil above it for coolness? It weathered through the years of the silent underground railroad, and no one spoke of its enduring presence. That stage is worthy of restoration.

Retrieving this view is a surprise to the writer and, perhaps, for the reader too. It marks an unmentioned history in the backdrop of the Appalachian plateau. Are we to walk through the undergrowth now protecting this site? Hidden from view, but restored in the memory caches of many people.

This memory of grace caught on the tip of nighttime silence by a surprised soul.

DRIFTING

Drifting into the soft tide of sleep like a thin piece of driftwood that reaches a far-away shore. Gentle in its weathering and untarnished by any of day's desires. Just drifting like an even rhythm of non-composed music. The waves begin to rise, drifting into nothingness. The sands of time welcome the new addition to its own little picture.

Drifting into the shades of sleep within the folds of peace. Gifts bestowed by the Great Master of Life upon the eternal soul. There's a deep silence within us in the company of rhythm and wind.

Drifting with timeless wholeness of the unexpected, into dreams imparted without any stress. Just moments metered into heaven's clock that angels hold. This drifting is the soul-touching element that recharges us for the incoming day.

Glorious pieces of life in ascent and descent as the ladder of time extends upward.

Eternal praise for peaceful drifts in my life! Sharing these words of Love with you.

Drifting...Daring...Sharing!

WALTZING THOUGHTS

Relax with the waltzing music, and let your heart catch its rapture.

Romantic feelings sift into the day's timeless, rhythmic music filling the spheres, unclouded by any past recall. Words fill the little cracks in thought like warming by a long ago fireplace. No pain or fear can be a part of this moment now. This perfection is the mystical embrace with a peace-holding time. Musical notes apply healing balm on every listening soul. Rapids stream along in hearty relishing of

rocky terrain, and splashes end in a pool of quiet. Have you ever found this retreat from worry, fret or concern?

Take hold of a rubber tube and enjoy the current toward fulfillment. Life's purpose may be discovered in the pool of quiet. The discovery is that the pool exists on a higher, not lower, plateau. The quest is an adventure initiated through Power Steering.

Waltzing thoughts and harmony shared!

HEART OF TIME 2

Within the pulse-beat of time, unmeasured by human clock, is an all-knowing within Higher Power.

We needn't worry about this within human breast, as Higher Power holds the length of destiny. To wonder is good, because awareness brings a focus to purpose. We rise above the everyday calendar page into the satisfaction of reaching for the best.

Focus shows in our eyes, and we note it clearly in the penetrating interest of others. In each day we find special guides, sometimes when a door is opened by strangers, or when appear familiar faces from past experiences. The exchange is a quality immeasurable in delight. There's a destiny touch as a reminder of right place and time.

The impulse to judge is not on the calendar. It's the unexpected that again thrives within hearts.

Thank you, Lord, for preserving breath and heart to give energy.

KEEPING ON 2

The page of time keeps beckoning us on. We leave behind weathered lines that were written to speak, but their directed purpose extends the original heartbeats of pounding joy.

Penning the design of purpose tunes senses to great surprise! Then letting go and keeping on wrap wonderful gifts for those who come later. And each one of us is a human work of art for the world to discover insights when they look inside the wrapping.

Purpose, plan and destiny and how these are discovered are delivered in unmapped wireless messages. Sensitivity is the key to unlocking these turning points in soul growth. Feelings of grace have no timeline in arriving or departing.

Just keep on with the hand of willingness to share. Perhaps sharing is the biggest lesson to learn on earth's journey.

Keeping on: a challenge for each day to make the world lighter, brighter and more beautiful in re-creation.

DEDICATION TO LIFE

When the orbital path is set, the mission is infused with anticipation, excitement and wonder.

Creativity is the ignition propellant behind the plan to reach the planets and other destinations of the heavens.

Oxygen and free speech mix for dedication to life. Fragile we are, but determined to build a station with higher purpose. The ship becomes a lighthouse in the sky, and the stars are twinkling sky lights for "Peace on Earth."

Intellect is the launch site for flight paths of discovery of human potential, paths not previously explored.

And dedication to life - a longevity thread of gold.

STARDUST

Have you ever thought that Stardust may surround each of us?

The discovery of thought was found in a Mindfulness Class, and it was expressed in a written sharing. It stuck in the memory and returned, leaving an impression of deep appreciation. The novel was hidden on a quiet library shelf. It was so indelible that it required more than a passing nod.

Stardust is everywhere. It is just not recognized until thought is given space to shine. A legacy so delicate that ancestors left their earth-bound footsteps behind for us to find.

Stardust is also a freeze-frame of a moment in time, like a time capsule to be dug up for hidden treasures to insure legacy. Stardust leaves traces that connect the past and present with the future. Stardust can be found in the eyes of excited children or in the weathered faces of retiring seniors. It's in the eyes of the soul speaking and in the breaths of enduring love. If you take the time to absorb the silence, you see stardust, and you comprehend the beauty of the gifts that have been bequeathed to you.

It just might be found sitting on a mantel, in a vase of flowers, or in a very old bible that needs a new binding. Could it be in a leather covering of *Pilgrim's Progress*? It's timeless, enduring and unfathomable in depth.

A Song: "Breathe on me, breath of God!" The label must be recognized as precious.

Set your starting marker at the beginning of your stardust trail.

MENU

"Hey, Lord!" No disrespect intended!

But I'm still awake, and it's 1:00 a.m.!

I've fed my body with food: half a banana, crackers and some peanut butter.

I've consoled my mind with quiet. I've allowed the soul to reach out and speak, a little muffled, but that's a rather deep undertaking. Why is rest so far away in this new day?

Oh! Teaching me patience! I know you are smiling with this recognition finally taking center stage.

Deep breaths and lifting of the shoulders: Does this mean that the weight of understanding is light? Intuitive moments, when the ignition key turns on the Power Steering of beginning again.

St. Benedict said, "Always we begin again."

In this, the home stretch of the freeway of learning, I'll just have to send you a signal of SOS for a little life preserver as an attachment file to my prayer.

What menu page should the cursor click?

UNLIMITED

Put the brakes on going in reverse and roll on toward the unlimited life! It isn't chronology that spoils the beauty of progress; rather, it is the negativism of people who put the limited guages on your life.

So look in the mirror, laugh at the reflection, and it will show the real you. See the unlimited self that climbs high mountains of experience and loves the view from the top. Don't give up the adventure because someone tells you not to take a stairway that leads you up.

"Unlimited" may be a business license. But it can also be your own personal life with unlimited miracles of expression. It's a journey with very few sign posts or stoplights, because you are the map maker charting the course of choices.

The freedom of joy turns off the windshield wipers. There is no need for those anymore. You can see clearly now! No fog inhibits you. The way lies open. The direction, place and distance are yours to own. Wow!

Write your own Unlimited Story! Share it with others. This author's words are few. They are for giving you time to write your own script. Don't scrap it now. Do it now!

Good luck and blessings in whatever language you speak, think and pray. Thanks to Power Steering, you are Unlimited!

Acknowledgements

The success of Power Steering 2 is shared first with genuine appreciation to my friends for their many expressions of encouragement and enthusiasm for this project. I always find joy in the staunch support of my family, professional colleagues and individuals who inspire me to stay on chart. I feel blessed by the wonderful opportunities to be in the right place at the right time to recognize and share my intuitive experiences. Specifically, I would like to thank:

Daniel Wetta of Daniel Wetta Publishing, my editor and publisher, who, besides being a social media specialist and author in his own right, is a mentor for me.
Brenda Womack, Executive Assistant.
Anne Silar, Senior Editor, Women of Distinction Magazine.
Neal Steele, WXGM Extra 99.1 FM, Gloucester, Virginia.
Bethany Emerson, Marketing Specialist and Consultant.
Cathy Leach, Writer's Council associate and Virginia Regional Ballet professional.
Donna Dodd, Virginia real estate professional.
Women of Distinction Magazine for reviews and publication.
Christopher Wren Association of The College of William and Mary, Williamsburg, Va., where I have enjoyed their courses in life-long learning.
The Chesapeake Bay Writers and the Williamsburg Writers Gathering.

About the Author

The thirst for expression began at an early age when learning to read and write was a great accomplishment. Receiving approval from the German writing teacher who expected perfection of letter forms by keeping the hand in her style of wrist-straight and wearing a penny for discomfort.

I reached for creativity after experiencing feelings of wonder about my huge old Victorian home built in great logs by Scottish ancestors in the edges of the 1700's. Family relics in the home suggested fascinating stories that echoed among the walls and great cathedral ceilings.

My pursuit of excellence was early rewarded when I won a contest of patriotism in an American-Legion-sponsored event with the theme, "What Democracy Means to Me!"

Then came early years of dancing and singing, followed by years in church as a director of congregational singing. Drama, too, entered the stage, but this soon disappeared when a library filled with books fueled my contagion.

You ask, "Where did this all begin?" For me, growth was an untamed progression that finally found discipline and meaning through the art of writing.

The titles of positions would fill a page in experiencing the various opportunities that schooling offered. Skipping the shorthand and speed-reading and entering with peers into the business field turned out to be a mistake: All the little facets of education caught on from friends who were college-bound. Leadership roles weren't then identified. One just rolled right through. Nothing special, those years, they were just a natural evolving of energy.

I had another passion - to capture life on film of cameras. This was a concealed treasure in the heart of a country girl who had great aspirations. It gave me impulses to explore the next village over, with its uptown fashion-design stores.

Education seeped through the very cells of the author. Each new course in psychology and sociology and education, all requirements for teaching, became for me its own book of adventures. Pursuing education became a lifelong journey. There is no need to expose the great length of time and effort in achieving degrees. For me, the precious encounters and dramas remain in memories, free vitamins to take at any time.

So what title would best describe this author of the 21st Century? Just call me blessed, fortunate beyond wildest dreams, with education, authorship, photographic moments, and family and friends! This all winds up to be a little profile of M. J. Scott (USA). Traveling and writing are the very essence of living on top of the mountain.

www.ingramcontent.com/pod-product-compliance
Lightning Source LLC
Chambersburg PA
CBHW060800050426
42449CB00008B/1464